Dedication

This book is dedicated to the many tourists, visitors, retired folks and Arizona natives who enjoy the fantasy, scenery, recreation and the superior cooking from the Great Canyon State.

© Copyright Applied For 1992 by Wes Medley
All rights reserved. No part of this publication may be reproduced, stored in a retrieval system, or transmitted in any form or by any means, electronic, mechanical, photocopying, recording, or otherwise, without the prior written permission of Original Western Publications, 214 High Street, Box 530, Cairo, Nebraska 68824, Phone (308) 485-4284.

Cover Design: Wes Medley and Angela Coombs
Illustrations: Carol Trumler
Layout: Marilyn Oseka and Shirley Wooden
Publisher: Wes Medley
Printing: Record Printing Co., Cairo, NE 68824

About the Author

Wild Wes is a former rodeo champion who had a reputation for also being a well-known Western cook who cooked for many rodeos, ranches, organizations and restaurants. Wild Wes spent the better part of 10 years collecting Arizona's legendary recipes. He is the well-known author of <u>The Original Cowboy Cookbook.</u>

"Wild Wes" Medley
Rodeo Champion

Quote from Wild Wes...

"It's for sure I'm no author, but I was encouraged to write this Arizona Cookbook by a lot of friends and acquaintances in the Great Canyon State of Arizona that I had shared my recipes with and had cooked for.

It took me a better part of 10 years to obtain these Arizona recipes.

These recipes were written down on napkins, feed bags, paper pokes and on the back of tobacco pokes, and most anything I could find to write on when I didn't have proper pen and paper.

I want to thank all you folks who buy this book and I guarantee this will be the best eatin' you ever stuck a fork and spoon into."

Your's for good eatin',
Wild Wes Medley

Table of Contents

Regional Ranch & Pioneer Cooking 5

Mexican & Indian Cooking 39

Bar-B-Q and Chili 63

Breads & Sweets 85

**Sauces, Gravies, Preserves,
   Canning & Relishes** 101

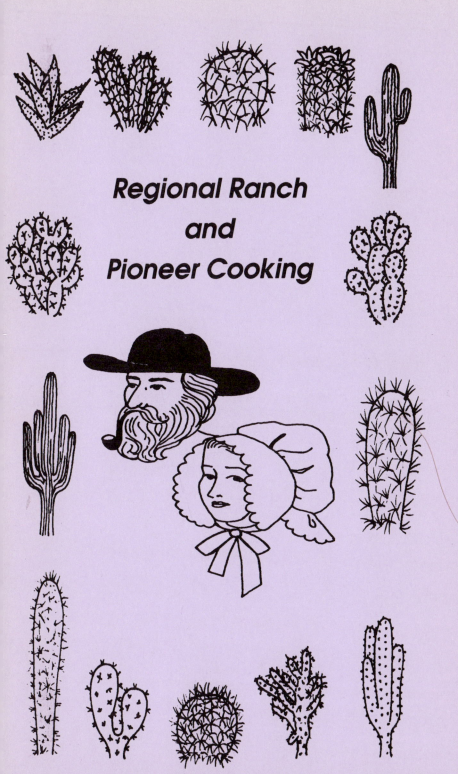

REGIONAL RANCH & PIONEER COOKING

ARIZONA APPLE DUMPLINGS

Rich baking powder
Biscuit dough
6 apples, medium size
1/2 c. brown sugar
1/2 tsp. salt
1 tsp. cinammon
1 tsp. nutmeg
1/2 c. raisins
2 T. butter

Prepare biscuit dough, roll 1/4" thick and cut into squares. Pare and core apples and place one in center of each square. Fill each with a portion of the seasonings, sugar, raisins and dot with butter. Bring corners of the dough to the top of the apples and seal by pricking with a fork. Bake at 375 degrees for 30 minutes. Serve with cream or milk.

BAKED SPARERIBS WITH SAUERKRAUT DUMPLINGS

Spareribs
Sauerkraut
2 c. flour
1 egg beaten
1 tsp. baking powder
1 c. milk

Cut spareribs into serving portions and place in the bottom of roasting pan. Add the sauerkraut and a little liquid. Cover and bake in moderate oven, 350 degrees, for 1 1/2 hours. Make dumplings by combining flour, baking powder, milk and egg. Drop by spoonfuls in sauerkraut; cover tightly and bake 20 minutes.

ARIZONA FARM PANCAKES

3/4 c. flour
1 T. sugar
1 c. dairy sour cream
4 eggs
1 c. small curd cottage cheese

Sift flour and sugar into a mixing bowl. Blend in sour cream. Beat eggs until light and fluffy. Fold into flour-sugar-cream mixture along with cottage cheese. Bake on a greased griddle on each side until golden brown. Serve with hot melted butter and hot strawberry or blueberry sauce.

ARIZONA HUSH PUPPIES

1 1/2 c. white cornmeal
1/2 c. unsifted all-purpose flour
1 tsp. salt
1 tsp. baking powder
1/2 tsp. baking soda
3/4 c. buttermilk
1 egg, beaten
1/2 tsp. Tabasco sauce
16 ozs. oil or lard

In medium bowl, mix cornmeal, flour, salt, baking powder and baking soda. Stir in buttermilk, egg, and Tabasco; mix well. Drop by tablespoons into oil that has been heated to 375 degrees in a deep fryer. Fry until light brown, about 2 to 3 minutes. Remove and drain on paper towels.
Yield: About 20 Hush Puppies

ARIZONA MOLASSES TAFFY

1 1/4 c. sorghum or dark molasses
1 T. vinegar
1 T. butter
3/4 c. sugar
1/8 tsp. soda
1/8 tsp. salt

Combine sorghum, sugar and vinegar and cook to 270 degrees or to the soft crack stage. Stir occasionally to prevent burning. Remove from heat; add butter, soda, and salt. Stir enough to blend. Pour into buttered pans. When cool enough, gather into a ball and pull between ungreased fingertips until firm and light in color.

ARIZONA TERIYAKI STEAK WITH ONIONS

1 1/2 lbs. beef steak
1/2 c. soy sauce
1/4 c. dry white wine
2 T. brown sugar
1 tsp. ginger
2 cloves garlic, minced
1 lg. sweet onion, sliced
1 T. butter

Combine soy sauce, wine, brown sugar, ginger and garlic. Place steak in plastic bag; add marinade, turning to coat. Tie bag securely and marinate in refrigerator 6 to 9 hours or overnight, turning at least once. Drain marinade from steak; reserve. Broil steak to doneness desired. Meanwhile, cook onion in butter in frying pan until soft. Stir in 1/4 cup reserved marinade. Cook 4 to 5 minutes. Slice steak and serve with onions.

ARIZONA BOILED TONGUE

For **fresh beef tongue,** scrub well; cover with boiling water and bring to a boil. Skim, cover and simmer until tender, about 3-4 hours. Add **1/2 tsp. salt per lb.** when partly cooked. Cook tongue in salted water until tender and add seasoning to taste. Remove skin and return to water. One hour before serving, put into deep roasting pan. Pour over sauce given next. Cover and bake 30 minutes, turning often.

SAUCE FOR BOILED TONGUE

2 c. strained water (in which tongue has been boiled)
1 1/2 c. stewed tomatoes
4 T. Worcestershire sauce
1 can mushrooms
Salt and pepper
Flour
Butter

Add gradually the strained water in which the tongue has been boiled, the stewed tomatoes, Worcestershire sauce, mushrooms and salt and pepper. Blend flour and butter to thicken sauce.

DESERT CHICKEN FRIED STEAK WITH COUNTRY GRAVY
"An Arizona classic"

2 pounds round steak, tenderized, trimmed of all fat
1 c. flour
Salt and pepper
2 eggs, slightly beaten
1/2 c. milk
Oil for frying
COUNTRY GRAVY:
6 T. bacon or pan drippings
6 T. flour
3 c. hot milk
Salt and pepper

Cut steak in 6 pieces. Combine flour, salt and pepper. Dredge steaks in flour mixture to coat. Combine eggs and milk. Dip steaks in egg mixture, then dredge again in flour. Heat oil in heavy skillet. Place steaks in hot oil and fry until golden brown on each side.

Prepare gravy: Remove steaks and keep warm. Leave 6 tablespoons of pan drippings in skillet. Add flour, cooking and stirring until flour browns. Add hot milk and stir to thicken. Season with salt and papper to taste. Pour over warm steaks. Serves 6.

FLAVORFUL BEEF AND BLACK BEAN SALAD

1 lb. boneless sirloin steak, cut 1-in. thick
1/2 c. fresh lime juice
2 T. orange juice
1 T. brown sugar
2 T. olive oil
1 T. chopped fresh thyme
1 clove garlic, minced
1/4 tsp. red pepper flakes
1 lg. orange
1 (15 or 16-oz.) can black beans drained and rinsed
2 green onions, including green top, thinly sliced
4 c. sliced Romaine lettuce, cut 1/4 in.

Trim excess fat from beef top sirloin steak. Combine 6 tablespoons lime juice, orange juice, brown sugar, 1 tablespoon oil, thyme, garlic and pepper flakes. Place steak in plastic bag and marinade, turning to coat. Close bag securely and marinate in refrigerator 30 minutes. Remove steak from marinade; discard. Place steak on rack in broiler pan so surface of meat is 3 to 4 inches from heat. Broil 16 to 20 minutes for medium-rare, turning once. Carve steak into 1/8-inch slices. Meanwhile peel orange; cut into 1/2-inch thick slices. Separate each slice into sections. Combine orange with beans, green onions, remaining lime juice and olive oil. Arrange romaine on 12-inch platter; spoon bean mixture on top lettuce around edge. Place beef in center of platter. Serve with fresh tomato salsa. 4 servings.

Preparation time: 25 minutes; Marinating time: 30 minutes; and Cooking time: 16 to 20 minutes.

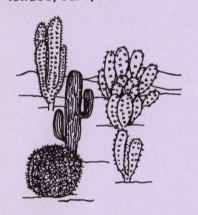

GRAND CANYON STEAK

12 oz. can beer
1/2 c. chili sauce
1/4 c. salad oil
3 T. soy sauce
1 T. Dijon mustard
1 tsp. Tabasco
1/8 tsp. liquid smoke, optional
1/2 c. onion, coarsely chopped
2 cloves garlic, minced
3 lbs. sirloin steak, 1 1/2" to 2" thick
Salt and pepper

Mix all ingredients except steak, salt and pepper. Simmer 30 minutes. Brush steak with sauce.

Grill steak 4 inches from medium-hot coals for 15 minutes on each side, basting frequently with sauce. Season with salt and pepper to taste. Serve hot with sauce. Serves 6 to 8.

GREEN PEPPER STEAK

1 lb. beef top round steak, cut into 1/4 " strips
1/4 c. soy sauce
1 clove garlic, minced
1 1/2 tsp. fresh ginger, grated or 1/2 tsp. ground ginger
1/4 c. salad oil
1 c. thinly sliced green onions
1 c. green peppers, cut in 1-inch squares
2 stalks celery, thinly sliced
1 tsp. cornstarch
1 c. water

Pour over meat the combination of the soy sauce, garlic and ginger. Marinate for 1 hour. Heat oil in large skillet. Add beef and brown. If not tender, cover and simmer for a few minutes over low heat. Turn heat up, add vegetables and toss until tender, about 10 minutes. Mix cornstarch with water and add to pan. Stir and cook until thickened. Serves 4.

HOMER'S IRON SKILLET SPECIAL

1 lb. dry pinto beans
6-lb. beef rump roast
1 T. lard or shortening
1 c. banana pepper or green pepper strips
2 sliced medium onions
2 c. tomato juice
1 8-oz. can tomato sauce
1/2 c. water
2 T. cider vinegar
2 T. brown sugar
2 tsp. salt
1 tsp. dry mustard
1 tsp. thyme

Wash beans; cover with cold water and let soak overnight. Bring beans to a boil and cook 1 hour; drain, discarding water. Brown roast in hot fat in a large Dutch oven or roaster. Add peppers and onions; cook until tender. Add beans and remaining ingredients. Cover and bake in 350 degree oven for 2 1/2 to 3 hours or until beans are tender and meat is done. Will serve 10 hungry cowboys.

RODEO PORK WITH ONIONS

2 I-lb. pork tenderloins, cut in julienne strips
6 med. onions, chopped
1/2 c. cooking oil, divided
1 tsp. salt
1 tsp. paprika
3/4 tsp. pepper
1/14 tsp. crushed red chilies
1 or 2 sweet red peppers, cut into long strips
Feta cheese (optional)

Saute onions in 1/4 c. oil in skillet 2-3 minutes. Stir in spices. Place on low heat to keep warm. In separate skillet, brown pork in remaining 1/4 c. oil. Cook over medium heat 15-20 minutes. Top with pepper pieces. Cover and simmer 5 minutes. Stir onion mixture into meat. Garnish with 1 inch cubes of Feta cheese, if desired. Serves 8.

*Rodeo, 1950, Phoenix Stockyard Restaurant

SALOON BEANS
(Best Darn Beans in the State)

1 1/2 qt. dried red beans
1/2 lb. salt pork
2 lg. onions, cut up fine
1 1/2 c. lard or other cooking fat
Several dried red Mexican chili peppers
1/2 lb. round steak
1 can green chilies or 3 fresh fried chilies
1 clove garlic
Salt to taste

Wash and clean beans. Soak overnight in warm water, no salt. Add pork, onion and lard and cook until beans get tender. Cook red chilies in small amount of water until tender. Work through a colander. Fry round steak in its own suet. When well done, put through meat grinder. Add garlic, red and green chilies, ground meat to the beans. Cook over low heat long enough to mingle all flavors.

SOURDOUGH STEAK

1"-thick round steak (about 3 lbs.)
1 c. all purpose-flour
2 tsp. onion salt
2 tsp. paprika
1 tsp. black pepper
1 c. Sourdough Starter (see Sour Dough recipes under "Bread" category)
3/4 c. lard or shortening

Using a meat tenderizing mallet or knife, pound steak to 1/2 inch thick. Cut into serving pieces. Combine flour and seasonings. Dip pounded steak in Sourdough Starter, then in flour mixture. Fry in 1 inch of hot lard in heavy skillet. Makes 6-8 servings.

CANYONLAND'S CABBAGE

1 1/2 lb. bacon
2 bell peppers, chopped
1 onion, chopped
4 heads cabbage, cored and quartered, (do not shred)
1 10-oz. can Renown tomatoes and chilies with cilantro
10 oz. water
Salt and pepper, to taste
Lemon pepper, to taste

In a large, heavy pot, place minced bacon and brown over medium-high heat. To this mixture, add peppers and onion and saute. Add cabbage, tomatoes, water and seasonings. Bring to a boil. Lower heat and simmer for 20 minutes, stirring occasionaly. Serves 10 to 12.

CHICKEN LIVERS WITH APPLES AND ONIONS

3/4 lb. chicken livers
3 T. flour
1/2 tsp. salt
1/4 tsp. pepper
3 med. sized apples
1/4 c. vegetable oil
1/4 c. sugar
1 lg. onion, thinly sliced

Rinse chicken livers and drain. Coat livers evenly with a mixture of flour, salt and pepper. Set aside. Wash and remove cores from apples. Cut apples into 1/2 inch slices, to form rings. Heat 2 Tablespoons oil in a frying pan over medium heat. Add sliced apples and cook until lightly browned. Turn slices carefully and sprinkle with sugar. Cook, uncovered, over low heat until tender. Remove from pan and reserve. Heat remaining 2 Tablespoons oil over low heat. Add chicken livers and onion rings. Cook over medium heat, turning mixture often to brown all sides. Serve with apple rings. Serves 4-6.

DESERT RICE

1 lb. chicken livers or giblets, chopped (I usually use gizzards)
1 lb. sausage
1 c. onion, chopped
1 bunch green onions, chopped, optional
2 T. chopped parsley, optional
1/2 c. celery, chopped
1 clove garlic, chopped
1/2 tsp. basil
Salt and pepper to taste
Hot sauce to taste
1 10 3/4 oz. can chicken broth
1/2 tsp. thyme

Saute giblets and sausage until tender. Add onion, parsley, celery, green onion and garlic. Cook slowly until tender. Add thyme, basil, rice, salt, pepper, hot sauce and chicken broth. Cook over medium heat until hot, stirring constantly. Yields about 8 servings.

ETHEL'S STEWED CHICKEN AND DUMPLINGS

1 stewing hen (4-6 lbs.)
4 c. water
2 stalks celery, chopped
3 peppercorns
1 carrot, chopped
1 med. onion, chopped
2 tsp. salt
DUMPLINGS
1 c. flour
2 tsp. baking powder
1/2 tsp. salt
2/3 c. milk
1 T. melted butter
1 T. chopped parsley

Clean chicken and cut into pieces. Place in a kettle with water, celery, carrot, salt and peppercorns. Bring to a boil, then reduce heat and simmer 15-20 minutes. Remove surface broth and scum. Let chicken simmer 2 hours or until meat is tender. (Add more water, if necessary.)

Combine dumpling ingredients until just moistened and drop by spoonfuls into the slowly boiling chicken broth. Cover kettle and let dumplings cook 12-15 minutes. Place chicken pieces on a serving plate or platter and arrange dumplings around them.

*Bill, Arizona, T & T Ranch, 1914

HOTEL TURKEY CASSEROLE

1/2 c. sliced mushrooms
6 T. butter
1 T. flour
2 1/4 c. turkey broth
1/2 c. chopped, cooked celery
4 sliced water chestnuts
4 T. sherry wine
Salt to taste
1 pinch nutmeg, optional
5 c. cooked, diced turkey

Saute mushrooms in butter; drain and add flour to butter. Blend until smooth; add broth, celery, mushrooms, chestnuts, sherry and salt. Mix with turkey. Arrange in buttered casserole. Place in pan of water and bake at 400 degrees 25-30 minutes or until bubbling. Especially tasty with a topping of toasted almonds, sliced.

OLD SOUTH ARIZONA SPICED CHICKEN

1 broiler-fryer (2 1/2-3 1/2 lbs.) cut up
Salt
1/2 c. all-purpose flour
1/3 c. vegetable oil
1 med. onion, diced
1/2 c. chopped celery
1 c. catsup
1 c. water
1/4 c. lemon juice
3 T. Worcesterchire sauce
2 T. brown sugar
2 T. vinegar
1 small hot pepper
Cooked rice or noodles

Sprinkle chicken with salt. Dredge chicken in flour; brown in hot oil in a Dutch oven. Remove the chicken from Dutch oven. Drain off excess oil. Combine remaining ingredients except rice in Dutch oven; add chicken. Cover and bake at 350 degrees for 1 hour. Remove hot pepper; discard. Serve chicken mixture over rice or noodles.

PAPAGO ROAST PHEASANT STUFFED WITH GRAPES AND NUTS

3 lbs. pheasant, dressed and larded
1/2 tsp. thyme
1 T. salt
1/8 tsp. fresh ground pepper
3/4 c. butter
18 dried juniper berries, crushed
1 c. mixed broken nut meats (walnuts or any kind)

Remove any pinfeathers from the birds and singe off hairs. Melt the butter and mix in thyme, salt, crushed juniper berries and pepper. Rub the birds well inside and out with the seasoned butter. Mash half of the grapes, then mix with remaining seasoned butter. Stuff each bird very full, skewer openings shut and truss. Wrap remaining stuffing in aluminum foil. Place birds on a rack in an open roasting pan and roast in a very hot oven, 425 degrees, for 15 minutes. The foil wrapped stuffing can be placed in the roasting pan beside the birds. Baste with drippings, reduce heat to moderate, 350 degrees, and continue to roast for 30 minutes more, or until birds are tender. Baste every 10 minutes with drippings. Makes 4 servings.

ARIZONA SALAD

1/2 c. salad oil
1/4 c. cider vinegar
1 tsp. salt
1 tsp. garlic salt
Juice of 2 lemons
Lettuce, torn into pieces
1 avacado, chopped
1 purple onion, sliced
2 tomatoes, quartered

Mix oil, vinegar, salt, garlic salt and lemon juice together two hours before serving. Toss vegetables together and add the dressing.

PHOENIX STEAK

2-inch thick sirloin steak
 (about 3 lbs.)
1 T. black peppercorns
3/4 c. water
2 cloves garlic, minced
4 c. coarse salt

Trim excess fat from steak. Crack peppercorns coarsely and mince garlic. Press peppercorns and garlic into both sides of steak and let stand at room temperature for 1 hour. Make a thick paste of salt and water; cover top side of peppered steak with 1/2 the mixture. If cooking steak over coals, cover salt side with a wet cloth or paper towel and place salt side down on grill. (Cloth or paper holds the salt in place; will char as the steak cooks, but this does not affect the taste.) Cover top side with remaining salt mixture and another piece of wet cloth or paper towel. If broiling, put salt side up, 3 inches from heat. Put salt on other side of steak when it is turned. Cook 15 minutes on each side for rare, 25 minutes for medium rare. Remove salt before eating. Makes 4-6 servings.

Delicious when served with One Shot Sauce (see Sauces and Gravies category).

This recipe came from a hotel in Phoenix, Arizona where the cattle barons stayed. In my uncle's notes, it did not name the hotel.

CANYON SUGAR BEANS

1/2 c. brown sugar
1/2 c. tomato catsup
2 tsp. vinegar
2 tsp. chili powder
Dash of Worcestershire sauce
1/2 tsp. salt
1/2 tsp. pepper
2 cans beans with pork
1 lg. onion, sliced

Mix sugar, catsup, vinegar, chili powder, Worcestershire sauce, salt and pepper to a paste. Add beans and onion. Bring to a boil. Bake in a 325 degree oven for 1 hour or until sauce is thick.

DESERT LAND POTATO SALAD

4 lbs. potatoes
Salt
3 T. red wine vinegar
1/4 c. oil
Salt and pepper to taste
1/4 c. fresh parsley, chopped
1/2 c. celery with leaves, chopped
1/2 c. red onion, chopped
1/2 c. pimiento-stuffed Spanish olives, chopped
1/2 c. sweet pickles, grated
4 hard-boiled eggs, grated
1/3 to 1/2 c. mayonnaise
4 T. prepared mustard
Pinch sugar
Paprika

Boil potatoes in lightly salted water for 20 to 30 minutes until tender. Let potatoes cool slightly, then slice in 1/4-inch thick slices. Combine vinegar, oil, salt and pepper and parsley. Whisk to blend.

In a large bowl, place potato slices and add vinaigrette. Toss gently to coat potatoes. Cool to room temperature. Add celery, onions, olives, pickles and eggs. Blend. Combine mayonnaise, mustard and sugar. Gently fold into potato mixture. Cover and refrigerate. Place salad in large decorative bowl lined with lettuce and dust with paprika. Serves 6 to 8.

Always keep potato salad refrigerated until ready to serve to prevent spoilage.

OLD-RANCH-STYLE BEANS

2 c. pinto beans, soaked overnight
1/4 lb. or more salt pork
2 qts. water
1 or 2 cloves garlic
Salt and pepper

Frijoles (Spanish Beans)—Use the red or Spanish beans. Boil a cupful until soft, several hours before using, setting them aside to cool in the water they were boiled in. Put a tablespoon of sweet oil or very nice dripping into a frying pan. Add a small chopped onion and before it browns, add the beans with some of the water in which they were boiled. Season liberally with finely chopped chili peppers and salt. Heat in bowls and mash them as they cook. Can be served at any meal.

The common camp and kitchen recipe is just as valid today as when Tex Taylor sang: "The pinto bean is hard to beat, with dry salt in the pot, Frijoles? Well it's jes' the same, jes' give me what y'v've got."

PAPAGO SWEET POTATO CAKES

4 lg. sweet potatoes
3 eggs
1 1/2 tsp. salt
1/8 tsp. fresh ground pepper
1 T. cooking oil

Parboil the potatoes until tender; peel and mash them. Mix in the eggs, salt and pepper. Heat the oil on a large griddle until a drop of water sizzles; drop the potato batter from a large spoon, and brown on both sides. As you turn the pancakes, flatten them with a spatula slightly. Add more oil to the griddle as needed. This recipe will make about 15 cakes about 3 inches in diameter. Serve hot with butter and, if you like, honey. Makes 10-12 servings.

RANCH STYLE FRIJOLES
"Beans"

1 lb. dried pinto beans
1 lg. ham bone or 2 smoked ham hocks, cracked
2 onions, chopped
3 garlic cloves, minced
2 bay leaves
1 T. fresh Mexican oregano, finely chopped, or 1 tsp. dried leaf oregano, crumbled
1 to 2 tsp. ground cumin
3 T. chili powder
Pinch sugar
Pinch crushed red pepper flakes
Water, to cover
1 16-oz. can tomatoes with juice, broken up
1 to 2 canned jalapenos, to taste
Salt and pepper to taste

Rinse beans, discarding any bad ones and place in large pot. Cover with water and soak overnight or bring water to a boil, boil 2 minutes; remove from heat, cover and let beans soak one hour. Discard water, rinse beans with cold water and drain. Place beans in pot with all other ingredients. Bring to a boil, reduce heat until liquid barely simmers and simmer, partially covered for 3 to 4 hours, until beans are very tender. Add water or beer during cooking, as needed, to prevent sticking and scorching. Remove and discard bay leaves. Adjust seasonings while cooking, if necessary. Serves 6 to 10.

SCOTTSDALE BAKED CABBAGE

1 head cabbage
1 tsp. salt
1 T. butter
1 T. flour
1 c. cabbage juice
1 c. mayonnaise
1 c. fine bread crumbs
1/4 c. butter

Boil cabbage with salt until almost tender. Cut into 2 inch pieces. Set aside. Make white sauce by melting butter, stirring in flour and cabbage juice. Cook until slightly thickened. Fold in mayonnaise. Fry bread crumbs in butter. Mix white sauce with cabbage in baking dish. Sprinkle top with buttered bread crumbs. Bake covered at 300 degrees for 15-20 minutes (just enough to heat through).

NOTE: This may be prepared a day ahead.

ARIZONA KELLY'S 7-BEAN SOUP
(Probably the best Bean Soup you'll ever eat!)

7 kinds beans (your choice)

Rinse off beans and let soak in warm water for 1 1/2 hours. Rinse off meat (ham hocks, ham chunks, salt pork or whatever you want to use). Cook meat on high temperature with salt, pepper, onions, tomatoes, celery and bell peppers (only if you desire). Let cook while beans are cooking for 1 1/2 hours, then add beans to pre-cooked meat and let cook for 1 1/2 hours or until done.

The next day, if you have some left over, you can add rice and reheat until rice is done. Good served with Skillet-baked Corn Bread.

*Kelly was a cook for the 4-Bar T Ranch in Tucson, Arizona, 1840-1869(?). One weekend, all the cowboys went to town to raise a little hell. Kelly told them to be sure to bring home some beans. The boys got somewhat drunkened-up and brought home 7 different kinds of beans and poured them in the bean box. This made Kelly mad, but he cooked all the beans together anyway. The bean soup was so good that it made Kelly famous for his soup and he fixed it that way all the time!

ARIZONA POT STEW

1 1/2 lbs. lean stew beef
1 pt. water
Salt
1 sliced onion
Pepper
3 T. sugar
2 tsp. cinnamon
1 pt. tomato juice or tomatoes

Combine stew beef, water and salt. Cook slowly until tender, letting water decrease to about 1 cup. Add rest of ingredients and continue cooking over low heat, stirring occasionally to keep from sticking until red gravy (which you use to top off the mashed potatoes) begins to thicken. Cinnamon and sugar may be adjusted to individual taste.

*Steerhead Saloon at Show Low, AZ 1886

BEAN KETTLE SOUP

1 lb. navy beans
1 ham bone
2 qts. water
2 tsp. salt
2 peppercorns
1 onion, chopped
2 stalks celery, chopped
3 carrots, sliced
2 c. minced ham

Place beans in a large crock and cover with water. Soak overnight. In the morning, drain off water and place beans in soup kettle with 2 quarts fresh water, the ham bone, salt and peppercorns. Cook 2-3 hours over low fire until beans are tender. Add vegetables and ham. Cook over low heat until vegetables are tender.

COWBOY BEEF STEW AND DUMPLINGS

1/2 c. flour
1 1/2 tsp. salt
1 tsp. pepper
2 lbs. (1 1/2" cubes) beef stew meat
1/4 c. oil
3 med. onions
1/2 c. water
3 1/2 c. (1 lb. 12 oz. can) whole peeled tomatoes and liquid
1 beef bouillon cube
2 lg. crushed garlic cloves
2 T. soy sauce
2 tsp. sugar
1/2 tsp. nutmeg
1/4 tsp. crushed red peppers

Combine flour, salt, and 1/2 teaspoon pepper. Dredge stew meat with flour mixture; reserve remaining flour mixture. Heat oil in 8-quart Dutch oven. Brown meat in hot oil, turning frequently to brown evenly. Remove meat. Cook onions and reserved flour mixture in Dutch oven, about 5 minutes. Stir in tomatoes and liquid, water, bouillon cube, garlic cloves, soy sauce, sugar, nutmeg, red peppers and remaining 1/2 teaspoon pepper. Blend well. Stir in meat. Boil gently, partially covered, about 1 1/2 hours, or until meat is tender. Top with Corn Dumplings. Makes 6 servings.

GLOBE CHUCKWAGON BEAN SOUP WITH BEEF

1 lb. soup beans
1 soup bone with meat on it
2 tsp. salt
1/4 tsp. pepper
3 potatoes, diced
1/4 c. chopped onions
1/4 tsp. cloves
1/4 tsp. allspice

Soak beans overnight in water. Cook the soup bone with water until the meat is tender. Remove the bone; cut off the meat. Cook the beans in the broth until they are soft. Add the meat, potatoes, onion and seasonings. Simmer until the potatoes are soft. Drop in the dough balls and boil 5 minutes longer.

Make dough balls out of biscuit mix of your own choice.

FLAGSTAFF HUNTER'S STEW

6 T. butter
1/2 lb. green sour apples, sliced
3/4 lb. cooked beef, pork, or buffalo
Nutmeg
1/2 c. buttered bread crumbs
1/4 lb. onions, sliced
2 1/2 lbs. sliced potatoes, cooked
Salt and pepper, to taste
2 1/2 c. meat gravy or stock

Melt 3 tablespoons butter in heavy skillet and add onions; saute until golden brown. Remove the rings; melt remaining butter and saute apple slices. Take heat-proof casserole and lightly turning, careful to prevent breaking, layer with 1/3 potatoes, 1/3 meat, 1/3 onion rings and 1/3 apples. Season with salt, pepper and nutmeg. Repeat layers until all are used. Pour over meat gravy or stock. Top with buttered bread crumbs and bake in a moderate oven, 350 degrees, for 1 hour.

*I obtained this recipe from a "drunk" in Cody, Wyoming who said he was Buffalo Bill Cody's grandson. I ate this stew at his cabin which was cooked by an Indian squaw he lived with. I later found out he wasn't kin to Buffalo Bill, but it's darned good stew and can be either fixed with pork, buffalo meat or beef.

MORMON-STYLE BEEF SOUP WITH DUMPLINGS

1 soup bone
2 lbs. stewing beef
2 qts. water
Salt
1 1/2 c. flour
1 egg
1/2 c. milk
Pepper

Cook meat until tender and remove from the broth. Add water until you have 2 quarts of broth. Make dumplings by mixing beaten egg with milk into flour until about the consistency of pancake batter. Drop from teaspoon into the boiling broth to form small dumplings. Cook for 3-4 minutes.

MORMON-STYLE PORK POT PIE WITH DUMPLINGS

8 loin pork chops
2 qts. water
1 dumpling recipe
4 medium potatoes
1 lb. sausage in casing

Boil the pork chops in water for 1/2 hour. Add the potatoes cut in half and the sausage cut in 1 inch pieces. Cook until potatoes are almost done. Drop well-beaten dumpling dough into the boiling meat mixture; cover and cook 10 minutes.

ORIENTAL SALOON STEW

2 1/2 lbs. beef cubes (5 c.)
2 T. all-purpose flour
1 T. paprika
1 tsp. chili powder
2 tsp. salt
3 T. lard
2 sliced onions
1 clove garlic, minced
1 28-oz. can tomatoes
3 T. chili powder
1 T. cinnamon
1 tsp. ground cloves
1/2-1 tsp. dry crushed red peppers
2 c. chopped potatoes
2 c. chopped carrots

Coat beef in a mixture of flour, paparika, 1 teaspoon chili powder and salt. Brown in hot fat in a large Dutch oven. Add onion and garlic; cook until soft. Add tomatoes, chili powder, cinnamon, cloves and peppers. Cover and simmer 2 hours. Add potatoes and carrots; cook until vegetables are done, about 45 minutes. Makes 6-8 servings.

*Oriental Saloon and Cafe, Tombstone, AZ 1884- a favorite hangout for cowboys and outlaws. There was an average of 1-2 persons killed there per week. This recipe was obtained from a bartender and cook who worked there.

POOR COWBOYS STEW

4 lbs. cubed beef stew or
  2 lbs. beef
2 lbs. chicken
6 c. water
2 tsp. salt
Pepper
5 slices bacon
1 qt. tomatoes
1/2 c. chopped onions
1 c. cubed carrots
1/2 c. chopped celery
1 c. cubed potatoes
1/2 c. chopped green pepper
1/4 tsp. crushed red pepper
1/2 clove garlic, minced
2 cloves
1 bay leaf
3 ears corn
1 pt. butter beans
1/2 c. flour

Combine meat, water, salt and pepper; cook until meat is tender. Fry bacon, retaining grease, and crumble. Add tomatoes, onions, carrots, celery, potaotes, green and red peppers, garlic and spices. Simmer at least 1 hour; remove bay leaf and cloves. Crush and add corn and undrained beans. Simmer 30 minutes. Blend flour and bacon grease; add to pot and simmer and stir until Burgoo thickens. Add additional salt, if necessary. Garnish with parsley and crumbled bacon.

RED RIVER BEAN SOUP

1 lb. dry pinto beans
2 1/2 qts. water
1/2 c. chopped onion
1 clove garlic, minced
1 lg. piece bacon rind
1 T. chili powder
1/2 tsp. oregano
1 4-oz. can peeled, seeded,
  diced green chili pepper
2 tsp. salt

Wash beans and soak overnight in cold water; drain. Put beans in a large kettle. Add 2 1/2 quarts water and simmer 1 hour. Add onion, garlic, bacon rind, chili powder, oregano and chili peppers. Cover and simmer 2 hours, adding salt the last hour. Makes 6 servings.

SHEEPHERDER'S BROWN POTATO SOUP

4 lg. potatoes
1 onion, chopped fine
1 qt. milk
Salt and pepper
1 T. butter
4 T. flour
1 hard-cooked egg

Dice potatoes and cook with the onion in salted water until tender. Add milk and bring to a boil. Brown flour in melted butter in a heavy frying pan, stirring constantly until well browned. Stir into the soup and boil a few minutes until thickened. Season to taste. Last, add the chopped egg.

I was helping a friend look for some lost horses around Powder River, Arizona. We came up on a sheepherder's cabin and he was nice enough to invite us in for a bowl of soup and bread. I wrote this recipe down on a piece of paper poke. Wished I'd written his recipe for his camp bread.

TRAIL WAGON BEEF SOUP

1 1/2 lbs. beef, cut into 1/2" pieces
4 T. flour
1 1/2 tsp. salt
2 twists ground black pepper (or 1 peppercorn)
3 T. cooking fat
1 can whole kernel corn
1 can red beans
2 c. chicken broth
1 1/2 c. water
1 clove garlic, minced
1 1/2 tsp. chili powder
1/2 tsp. hot pepper sauce
3 small onions, chopped
1/2 c. green pepper, chopped

Combine flour, salt, and pepper; dredge beef pieces. Brown beef pieces in the cooking fat in kettle or Dutch oven. Drain off drippings. Add corn liquid, bean liquid, but reserve corn and beans until later. Also, add chicken broth, water, garlic and chili powder. Cover kettle or Dutch oven and cook over low heat for 2 hours. Add onions and green pepper and cook 20 minutes. Add corn and beans; cook 10 minutes. Serve with corn bread and butter.

VENISON AND WILD RICE STEW

3 1/2 lbs. shoulder of venison, cut into 2" cubes
2 tsp. salt
1/8 tsp. fresh ground pepper
2 qts. water
2 yellow onions, peeled and quartered
1 1/2 c. wild rice, washed in cold water

Place the venison, water and onions in a large, heavy kettle and simmer, uncovered, for 3 hours or until venison is tender. Mix the salt, pepper and wild rice, cover and simmer for 20 minutes. Stir in mixture, then simmer, uncovered, for about 20 minutes more or until rice is tender and most of the liquid is absorbed. Makes 6-8 servings.

CANYON LAND MEATLOAF

4 lbs. lean ground beef
3 c. tomato sauce
6 oz. vegetable juice
1/4 tsp. rosemary
1 tsp. French herbs blend
1/4 tsp. black pepper
1/4 tsp. celery seeds
1/4 c. fresh parsley, minced
3 T. beef bouillon granules
3 onions
2 cloves garlic. minced
2 to 3 ribs celery with leaves
3 to 4 carrots, washed and scraped, cut in large diagonal slices

Mix ground meat with 2 1/2 cups tomato sauce. Add seasonings, using one teaspoon beef bouillon grandules. Finely chop one onion and add to mixture. Add garlic.

Shape into a loaf. Place in baking dish. Drizzle with additional tomato sauce. Add vegetable juice to pan. Sprinkle meatloaf with remaining beef bouillon granules. Quarter onion and surround meatloaf with it. Add celery and carrots.

Bake at 350 degrees for 1 1/2 hours, basting occasionally. Serves 6 to 8.

May use to stuff bell peppers or cabbage leaves. Bake to 350 degrees for 1 hour.

COOKSTOVE MEAT LOAF

1 lb. lean ground beef
1/4 lb. pork sausage
1 egg, beaten
1 T. butter, melted
3 slices bread, crumbled
1 onion, finely chopped
1 tsp. salt
1/8 tsp. black pepper
1/4 tsp. ground sage
1 beef bouillon cube
1/2 c. boiling water
4 strips raw bacon
4 T. chili sauce

Combine all ingredients except last four. Dissolve bouillon in the boiling water and add to mixture. Shape into a loaf and place in greased baking pan. Top with bacon strips. After meat has baked approximately 25 minutes, return to oven for remaining time. Bake in moderate (350 degrees) oven 45-50 minutes.

Bunk House, TZ Ranch, Globe, Arizona, 1926

GRAND CANYON MEATBALLS

3 lbs. lean ground beef or venison
1/4 c. soy sauce
2 T. minced onion
1/3 c. fresh parsley, snipped
2 cloves garlic, crushed
1/4 tsp. black pepper
2 to 3 T. oil
1 lb. can cranberry sauce
1/3 cup catsup
2 T. brown sugar
1 1/2 c. chili sauce
1 T. lemon juice

In a large bowl, combine meat, soy sauce, onion, parsley, garlic and pepper. Mix well. Shape into meatballs.

Brown in oil in skillet.

Combine sauce ingredients: cranberry sauce, catsup, brown sugar, chili sauce and lemon juice. Pour over meatballs. Simmer 30 minutes, turning often for suace to permeate meatballs.

Serve hot in chafing dish with toothpicks. Yield: 5 dozen.

PRESCOTT STUFFED GREEN PEPPERS

6 med. sized green peppers
1 lb. ground beef
1 T. olive oil
1 med. sized onion, minced
16 oz. can tomatoes, chopped
1/2 c. long grain rice
1 c. tomato juice
1 1/2 tsp. salt
1 T. chili powder
1/4 c. tomato paste
1/2 tsp. Tabasco sauce

Soak green peppers in ice water for 30 minutes. Slice off tops and remove seeds. Drop chilled, deseeded green peppers into boiling water, enough to cover, for 5 minutes. Drain and set aside. Heat olive oil in a large skillet and add remaining ingredients, stirring well. Cover and cook 10 minutes, stirring often. Remove from heat. Fill peppers with meat mixture and place in a greased baking dish. Bake at 375 degrees for 1 hour and 15 minutes. Serves: 6.

RANCH STYLE MEAT AND CABBAGE

1 lb. ground beef
1/8 tsp. pepper
1/3 c. uncooked rice
2 T. butter
1 can tomato soup
1 1/2 c. chopped celery
3 T. lemon juice
1 tsp. salt
1 1/4 tsp. salt
1 egg, beaten
6 lg. cabbage leaves
1 c. thinly sliced onions
1 1/4 c. water
1 tsp. minced parsley
1 tsp. sugar
1/8 tsp. pepper

Mix together lightly and thoroughly the ground beef, salt, pepper and egg. Mix in the rice. Cook the cabbage leaves in boiling, salted water until just tender. Drain. For the sauce, melt butter in a skillet. Add the onion and cook until tender. Blend in a mixture of the toamto soup and water. Add celery, parsley, lemon juice, sugar, salt and pepper. Simmer 10 minutes. To stuff cabbage leaves, place about 1/4 cup of meat mixture on the center of each leaf. Roll up each leaf, tucking the ends in toward center. Use wooden picks to fasten the leaves securely. Place the rolls in a large, heavy skillet. Pour sauce over rolls; cover pan tightly and cook slowly for 2 hours. Serve immediately.

COMPANY HAM

15 lb. sugar-cured Virginia ham, fully cooked
1 1/2 c. pineapple juice
1/2 c. prepared mustard
1/2 c. brown sugar
1/4 c. soy sauce
Whole cloves

Preheat oven to 325 degrees. Mix pineapple juice, brown sugar, soy sauce and mustard, blending smoothly. Trim ham of dark outer skin. Partially trim away fat, leaving 1/2" layer. Score fat in diamond pattern. Stud with whole cloves. Place in roasting pan, brush with glaze and bake 3 hours, basting frequently. Cover with foil, lower heat to 300 degrees and bake an additional hour.
Serves 10 to 12.

FLAGSTAFF SCRAPPLE

3 lbs. pork sausage meat, broken into fine bits
3 qts. water
1 lb. beef liver
Dried parsley
Sage
Poultry seasoning
Salt
Cornmeal

Boil pork sausage in 3 quarts water. Add beef liver, if desired. Cook until meat is very well done. (Do not taste pork mixture until finished cooking!) Add dried parsley, sage, poultry seasoning, and salt as desired. Stir moistened cornmeal into meat broth until thickened. Spoon into 5 loaf pans. Slice when cold into thin slices and put on baking sheet in 375-degree oven; turn once. Bake to delicate crispness. Serve with syrup. Can also be fried.

Steer Head Saloon and Cafe, Flagstaff, AZ, late 1800's. Recipe given to my uncle by a former cook there.

HERB-AND-GARLIC MARINATED LEG OF LAMB

1 c. olive oil
1 onion, sliced
1/3 c. dry white wine
1/3 c. fresh lemon juice
1/3 c. chopped fresh parsley
3 garlic cloves, minced
1 1/2 T. rosemary, crumbled
2 tsp. Dijon mustard
1/2 tsp. salt
1/2 tsp. freshly ground pepper
1/4 tsp. dried red pepper flakes
1 (5 to 6 lb.) leg of lamb, boned, butterflied and trimmed

Combine first 11 ingredients. Place lamb in large roasting pan. Pour marinade over. Cover lamb and refrigerate overnight, turning at least once.

Prepare barbecue grill with hot coals. Place lamb on grill and cook 15 minutes per side for rare, basting occasionally with marinade. Let stand 10 minutes before slicing and serving. Serves 6 to 8.

PIONEER RED EYE GRAVY

Fry up **salt-honey cured ham** in a large skillet; use amount depending on how many people you're going to feed. Fry over low heat until done. After meat is done, remove about 1/2 the grease from skillet along with the ham. Then add to the hot drippings about **1/2 c. or more coffee**, depending on how much ham drippings you have left over. Add **2 T. vinegar** and **1 tsp. to 1 T. brown sugar** and stir vigorously until gravy thickens. Some people add about 1 tsp. cornstarch to make it a little thicker. After gravy is done, serve with hot biscuits of your choice and the ham. Have plenty of coffee and water nearby, because it will sure make you thirsty!

1855-STYLE SAUCE

1 c. Southern Comfort (whiskey)
2 T. grated orange rind
1/4 c. honey
1/4 c. soy sauce
1 c. orange juice
2 cloves crushed garlic (or 1 tsp. garlic juice)
1 T. cornstarch

Combine. Pour into saucepan and bring to a boil and simmer for 12 minutes, stirring constantly. This sauce is perfect for turkey, ham, lamb or pork roast. Great with baked chicken. Double the recipe; let cool. Pour into small containers and freeze for future use at any time. Just heat and serve.

SPANISH OMELET

3 med. sized onions, thinly sliced
2 green peppers, thinly sliced and seeded
3 to 4 T. olive oil
1 tsp. chili powder
1/2 tsp. salt
1/2 tsp. pepper
1/2 tsp. Tabasco sauce
1 bay leaf
1/2 tsp. oregano
8 eggs, beaten
4 T. milk

Saute onions and green peppers in olive oil in a heavy skillet until tender. Sprinkle chili powder, salt, pepper, Tabasco sauce, bay leaf and oregano over sauted vegetables. Toss to blend. Simmer, stirring frequently, 5 minutes. Remove bay leaf and discard. Beat eggs with milk in large bowl. Pour eggs over vegetables, being very careful to keep vegetables in the center as much as possible. Turn only once and serve. Serves 4.

ARIZONA STOCKYARD SPECIAL HAM

Get **a first-quality ham**. A ham with a bone is preferred to a boned ham inasmuch as that flavors better. With a sharp knife, skin the ham back pretty well into the hock so that the ham can absorb as much sweetness as possible from the following syrup: Put enough **cold water and sugar** in kettle to cover ham (use 1 cup sugar for every quart of water). Stir sugar in the cold water until dissolved. Put ham in the cold sugar water and slowly bring to a boil. This will take about 1 hour. Boil about 10 minutes and shut off fire; remove from stove. Let ham soak and cool in the syrup for about 24 hours (48 hours is even better).

After this period, put the ham on the stove again in the same syrup and allow it to come to a boil. Simmer barely at boiling for about 12 minutes for each pound of ham. (Best size ham should be 11-14 pounds.)

After ham has boiled correct length of time, remove from hot syrup and place in a roaster. Stick **cloves** in fat side of ham about 1 1/2 inches apart and cover with 1/2 inch thick layer of brown sugar mixture made with **3 tablespoon sugar to 1 tablespoon flour.** Place in roasting pan; add **1 quart good dry red or white wine** and **2 cups sugar syrup.** Roast in slow oven at 300 degrees for about 3/4 hour. Baste ham at 10-minute intervals with wine.

SPECIAL HAM SAUCE

Take **2 cups liquid from a roast ham** after skimming most of the grease. Add **1 cup wine** to every 2 cups liquid and **1 teaspoon prepared mustard.** Stir into the liquid until well dissolved before the saucepan is put on the fire. Bring to a boil and add sufficient ordinary thickening made out of **flour and cold water** for proper consistency. Do not boil this sauce too long. Remove from fire; strain and serve after reaching desired consistency.

This recipe came from the old stockyards restaurant in Phoenix, Arizona. This type of ham was cooked by the lady cooks who worked in the cafeteria in this stockyard. A lot of ranchers just came to eat here instead of buying cattle. This is probably the best ham you can cook.

*One horn ranch, Cook Shack, near Willenburg, AZ. They used to call Shorty "Sweet Water Shorty". I have more of his recipes, but these four are my favorites.

BUNKHOUSE TURNIPS AND PORK

3 lbs. pork loin or
  boiling pork
3 lbs. sliced turnips
1 1/2 lbs. sliced potatoes
1 tsp. salt
1 T. sugar
Pepper, to taste

Boil pork loin or boiling pork in salted water to cover well done (several hours). Remove pork to baking pan; brown in oven at 350 degrees for 35 minutes. Have ready the sliced turnips and potatoes. Place in alternate layers in pork juice. Add salt, sugar and pepper to taste. Cook until tender. Serve with pork.

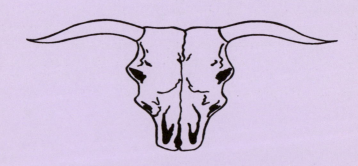

SHORTY'S SPARERIBS AND ROAST POTATOES
"Wild Wes's Favorite"

3 lbs. spareribs
1 tsp. salt
1/2 tsp. pepper
6 peeled potatoes

Bake spareribs in 350 degree oven for 1 1/2 hours or until all fat is drained and they have a crisp, brown color. Add salt and pepper. The last hour of baking, cut up potatoes lengthwise 1/2 inch thick slices. Lay on top shelf directly on the rack. When spareribs are crisp, potatoes will have a delightfully puffed-up brown cover. Butter adds zest.

SAUERKRAUT AND PORK

3-lb. piece pork loin
1 lg. can or carton sauerkraut
1 apple, peeled

Boil a piece of pork loin in water to cover for 2 hours or until well done. Remove pork to baking dish and bake at 350 degrees for 35 minutes or until nicely browned. Take juice from pork; add sauerkraut, then add apple. Simmer gently 1 hour. Serve with pork.
  NOTE: Leftover sauerkraut can be served with hot dogs and/or dumplings.

PIONEER HASH

1 lb. ground beef
3 lg. onions, about 3 1/2" in diameter, sliced
1 lg. green pepper, chopped
1 1-lb. can tomatoes
1/2 c. uncooked regular rice
1 to 2 tsp. chili powder
2 tsp. salt
1/8 tsp. pepper

Heat oven to 350 degrees. In large skillet, cook and stir ground beef until light brown. Drain off fat. Add onions and green pepper; cook and stir until onion is tender. Stir in tomatoes, rice, chili, salt, and pepper; heat through. Pour into ungreased 2-quart casserole. Cover and bake 1 hour.

Notes

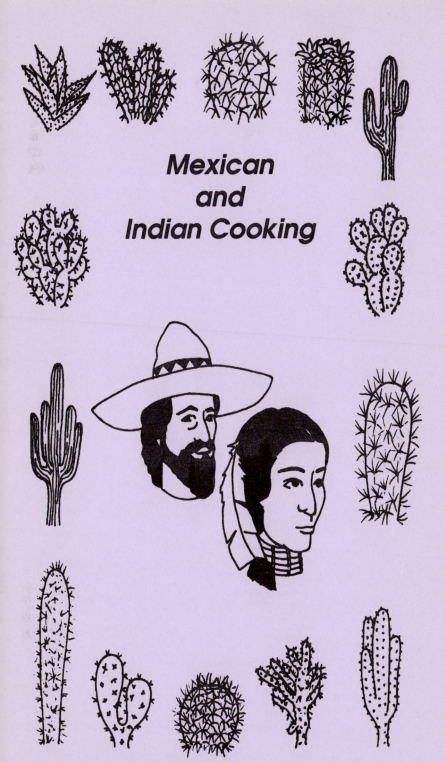

Mexican and Indian Cooking

MEXICAN & INDIAN COOKING

MEXICAN

ARIZONA'S BEST FAJITAS

5 lbs. fajitas (skirt steak) or flank steak
2 to 3 onions, sliced
Flour tortillas
Condiments
MARINADE:
1/3 c. oil
3/4 c. fresh lime juice
4 cloves garlic, minced
Salt to taste
1 T. lemon pepper
1 T. Worcestershire sauce
Dash Tabasco
1 jalapeno, finely chopped, optional

Combine oil, lime juice, garlic, salt, lemon pepper, Worcestershire sauce, Tabasco and jalapeno. Pour over meat and marinate for 3 to 4 hours prior to cooking.

Have butcher tenderize fajitas. Marintate as directed. Remove meat from marinade and grill over mesquite on hot grill until done. Grill 3 to 4 minutes per side for medium-rare, slightly longer for well done. Grill onions on a griddle over the coals. Prior to serving, slice fajitas diagonally across the grain as thinly as desired. Serve wrapped up in warm tortillas with grilled onions and your choice of condiments.

Serves 6 to 8.

Condiments: Pico de Gallo, picante sauce, guacamole, sour cream, grated Cheddar or Monterey Jack cheese.

BEEF MEXICANA

3 lbs. beef tenderloin
1 lg. onion, peeled, sliced
2 med. bell peppers, sliced
4 tomatoes, skinned, with seeds and juice removed
2 cloves garlic, crushed and chopped
Salt and black pepper to taste
1 c. tomato puree
3 T. sweet paprika
1 T. seasoned chicken stock base
2 to 3 chilies, serranos

Cut the tenderloin into 2-inch cubes and saute over very high heat in a little oil until the meat is browned on all sides but still rare in center. Remove from the pan and keep warm. In the same skillet, add a little more oil and saute the onions and bell peppers for 3-4 minutes until tender. Add the garlic; saute about 2 minutes more. Add the tomatoes and saute about 2 minutes. Stir in the tomato puree, paprika and chicken stock base. Season to taste with salt and pepper. Thinly slice the peppers, removing the skin and seeds. Toss the mixture together and return the sauteed beef to the pan. The meat should be resting in a layer on top of the vegetables. Heat the mixture through for about five minutes more, covered. Serve immediately. Delicious with plain white rice.

GAZPACHO

1/4 c. oil
2 T. lemon juice
6 c. tomato juice (1 lg. can)
2 c. beef bouillon (2 cubes in 2 cups water)
1 c. onion, minced
1 c. celery, minced
1 c. green pepper, minced
1 c. diced tomato
2 T. Worcesterchire sauce
1 T. salt

Beat oil and lemon juice together. Add all other ingredients. Refrigerate at least 3 hours before serving.

CHICKEN FAJITAS

5 whole boneless, skinless chicken breasts
3 T. oil
1/2 tsp. chili powder
1/2 tsp. ground cumin
Salt and pepper to taste
1 tsp. hot pepper sauce
One fresh lime, juiced
2 red bell peppers, seeded and cut in julienne strips
1 green bell pepper, seeded and cut into julienne strips
2 onions, thinly sliced
10 flour tortillas

Cut chicken lengthwise into 1/2-inch wide slices. Set aside. Combine oil, chili powder, cumin, salt and pepper, hot pepper sauce and lime juice. Mix well. Toss chicken slices in mixture until evenly coated. Cover, refrigerate and marinate several hours.

Over high heat, quickly brown fajitas and marinade, stirring to prevent sticking. Add red and green bell peppers and onions and cook briefly. Serve, topped with condiments of your choice, rolled up in steaming, soft flour tortillas.

Condiments may include shredded lettuce, fresh chopped tomato, sliced green onions with tops, shredded cheeses, sliced jalapenos, green and ripe olives, guacamole, sour cream and salsa.

ENCHILADAS, ARIZONA-STYLE

8 tortillas, corn
1/3 c. grated longhorn cheese
1/2 c. onions, chopped
1 T. fat
2 c. chile con carne

Heat fat and dip tortillas in one by one. Take out immediately. Dip the tortillas in the chile con corne. Fill tortillas with one-half the onion and cheese. Roll into thirds. Put enchiladas into shallow pan with seam side down. Cover with rest of onion and cheese and bake in 375 degree oven until cheese melts. Spoon hot chile con carne over enchiladas.

FIESTA

4 lbs. hamburger
3 onions, chopped
2 #3 can tomatoes
3 4-oz. cans tomato sauce
2 sm. cans tomato puree
2 1/2 T. chili powder
2 T. garlic powder
1 lg. can ranch style beans, not drained
2 lg. bags corn chips, crushed
1 lg. box instant rice, cooked
1 lb. Cheddar cheese, grated
Lettuce
Tomatoes
Onions, diced
1 jar green olives, chopped
2 ozs. pecans, chopped

Saute hamburger and onion, drain. Mix tomatoes, sauce, puree, powder, beans and simmer slowly as long as you like. Arrange your dishes of goodies as follows: Corn chips, instant rice, meat sauce, cheese, lettuce, tomatoes, onions, green olives and pecans. Serve with hot sauce and Doritos. Each of above arranged in separate dishes on your table and served buffet style. It is really good and not too expensive.

FRIJOLES (REFRIED BEANS)

1 lb. pinto beans
1 sm. can tomato sauce, optional
1 lb. onion, chopped
Longhorn cheese, grated, to taste
4 T. pure lard

Wash and clean beans. Let beans soak overnight in four quart pot. Cook slowly until tender, adding boiling water if necessary (cold water darkens beans). When beans are done, drain and save broth. Mash up beans to desired consistency and pour in 4 tablespoons of smoking-hot lard. Mix well, pour reserved broth back in, mix again and stir over low heat. Cover with optional tomato sauce, a layer of finely chopped onions and a generous layer of grated cheese. Cover pot and heat until cheese melts. Serve as a dip with tortilla chips or on Huevos Rancheros or chalupas.

GUACMOLE SENORA WIDENER

6 soft avocados (8, if small ones)
6 fresh green onions, minced
1 4-oz. can chopped green chilies
Garlic salt
Pepper
Squeeze of fresh lemon
2 to 3 tomatoes, sliced, optional
Lettuce leaves
Tortilla chips

Blend avocados, onions and chilies together, seasoning with garlic salt, pepper and lemon juice to taste. Serve on sliced tomatoes and/or lettuce leaves with tortilla chips as salad.

BEEF TACOS - TUCSON STYLE

1 1/2 lbs. hamburger
1 onion, diced
2 c. cooked potatoes (mashed coarsely)
1 can tomato sauce
Tortillas
Grated cheese
Shredded lettuce
Chopped tomatoes

Fry hamburger, set aside. Saute onion in hamburger drippings, draining off excess fat. Add one can tomato sauce, hamburger and potatoes. Mix.

Place one heaping tablespoon of mixture in center of corn tortilla. Press in place, drop in hot fat. Fold tortilla over to form cup. Cook until barely crisp. Drain on paper towel.

To serve: Fill cupped tortilla with grated cheese, shredded lettuce and chopped tomatoes. (Extra mixture may be refrigerated or frozen.)

JUST PLAIN 'OLE FAJITAS

1 to 1 1/2 lbs. beef skirt
2 T. season salt
1/4 T. garlic salt
1 lg. bell pepper
1/2 c. Worcestershire sauce
SAUCE
1 T. black pepper
1 med. onion
12 tortillas

Take beef skirt and wash under cool water. Place beef skirt in skillet that you will cook in. Cover top and bottom of skirt with season salt, then do the same with pepper. Shake garlic salt evenly on both sides. Take a fork and poke holes in skirt and pour the Worcestershire sauce over the skirt; let set 2 to 4 hours to marinate. After marinated, slice skirt into 1/4 inch slices. Turn range top on low and simmer for 45 minutes, stirring occasionally so it will cook evenly.

While skirt is cooking, slice onion and pepper and add to meat after 45 minutes. Cook vegetables with meat until tender. Warm tortillas in skillet or microwave. When mixture is ready, spoon into tortilla and roll together or let guests serve themselves. Serve with guacomole and salsa, if desired. Makes 12 Fajitas.

MEXICAN CHICKEN

4 lb. chicken
2 onions, chopped
2 sprigs thyme
2 sprigs fresh parsley
2 green bell peppers, chopped
1 red bell pepper, chopped
3 tomatoes, sliced
1/2 tsp. rosemary
1 garlic clove, crushed
Salt and black pepper to taste
1/4 c. soy sauce
Juice from one lime
8 T. oil
2 T. sugar

Cut up chicken. Place in shallow bowl and add onion, thyme, parsley, bell peppers, tomatoes, rosemary, garlic, salt and pepper, soy sauce and lime juice. Let stand 2 hours, turning to coat.

Heat oil in heavy skillet. Add sugar and let it brown and bubble. (This is the secret to the unique taste!) Add chicken and let it brown thoroughly, about 10 minutes, turing to brown evenly. Add marinade and cook on low heat, covered, until tender; about 45 minutes.

MEXICAN BEAN SOUP

1 T. bacon drippings
2 green onions, cut in 1-inch lengths
2 cloves garlic, minced
1 med. green pepper, coarsely chopped
1/4 c. tomato, peeled, seeded and chopped
1 tsp. dried coriander, crushed
1 c. pinto beans, cooked in water with garlic
3 c. bean broth
Salt to taste
GARNISHES:
1/4 c. onion, chopped
1/2 c. Monterey Jack cheese, grated

Saute onions, garlic and green pepper in bacon drippings until slightly soft, 3-5 minutes. Add tomatoes, beans and broth, coriander and salt. Bring to a boil and boil briskly, uncovered, for 10 minutes.

MEXICAN SALAD

1 sm. head lettuce
2 med. tomatoes
1 avacado (2 if sm.)
1 lg. sweet onion
1 c. Cheddar cheese, grated
1 16-oz. bag Fritos
1 8-oz. bottle sweet and spicy Catalina dressing

Use sharp salad knife and cut lettuce, tomatoes, avacado and onion into 1/2-inch squares as close as possible. Add cheese, Fritos and Catalina dressing. This is a delicious, nutritious treat! Good to take to parties to feed the kinfolks!

MEXICAN FIESTA

3 lbs. ground beef
2 onions, chopped
2 cans tomatoes
2 sm. cans tomato sauce
4 tsp. chili powder
1 tsp. garlic powder
1 lg. can Ranch Style beans
2 c. Minute Rice, cooked
2 lg. pkgs. Fritos
1 lb. cheese, grated
Lg. lettuce and tomato salad
1 onion, diced
1 can chopped black olives
1 jar green olives
Picante sauce, optional

Brown ground beef and onions. Drain grease. Add the rest of the ingredients and mix well. Cook 2 cups of Minute Rice. Set out meat sauce, rice, Fritos, cheese, lettuce/tomato salad, onion, chopped black olives and green olives. Let everyone "stack up" their own creation. Picante sauce is optional.

MEXICAN CORN TORTILLAS

3 c. Masa Harina
1 tsp. salt
1 1/2 T. fresh lard or shortening
3 c. boiling water

Mix Masa Harina and salt in a bowl. Melt lard in the boiling water. Stirring steadily, pour into bowl, until resulting dough is stiff. You can use a mixer, 2 or 3 minutes at medium speed. Scoop a lump of dough the size of an egg into the palm of one hand. Pat it round and thin to 5 inches in diameter. Or use rolling pin, putting dough between two pieces of plastic wrap. In the old days, damp muslin was used. Another option is the tortilla press, a hinged, metal gadget which works. Have griddle or comal hot and cook one minute per side until evenly light brown. Keep warm in a napkin if using at once. Wrap securely to freeze as they dry easily (but do not discard as they fry into corn chips or can be used in casseroles, broken). Yields: 18 6-inch corn tortillas.

MEXICAN WILD TORTILLA SOUP

3 to 4 corn tortillas
Oil for frying
2 tsp. oil
1/3 c. green onions with tops, sliced
4 c. seasoned chicken broth
1 1/2 c. boiled chicken breasts, skinned, deboned and cubed
1 10-oz. can Rotel tomatoes with green chilies
1 T. fresh lime juice
2 tsp. fresh cilantro, chopped
4 lime slices

Cut tortillas in strips, 1 X 2-inches. Fry in a small amount of oil until browned and crisp. Drain and reserve.

Heat 2 teaspoons of oil in skillet. Add onions and saute. Add broth, chicken and tomatoes with green chilies. Cover and simmer 20 minutes. Add lime juice.

To serve: Ladle into soup bowls and top with tortilla chips. Garnish with chopped cilantro and float a lime slice in center of each. Serves 4.

OLD STYLE ENCHILADAS OLE'

4 c. chili, heated
12 corn tortillas
1 lb. Cheddar cheese, grated
1/2 lb. Monterey Jack with jalapenos
or Swiss cheese, grated
1 or 2 onions, finely chopped
2 acocados, peeled, pitted and chopped
2 tomatoes, chopped

Heat chili. Heat oil in skillet. Quickly place tortillas, one at a time, in hot oil for 2 seconds, turning just to soften. Remove from oil and drain well on absorbent towels.

Place 3 tablespoon chili in center of each tortilla. Sprinkle liberally with mixed cheeses and onions. Roll up. Place in casserole, seam-side down. Top with additional chili and cheese liberally.

Bake at 350 degrees for 15 to 20 minutes until cheese is bubbly. Top with chopped avocados and tomatoes. Cover with foil to let steam.

Yield: 12 enchiladas

OLD-STYLE WHEAT FLOUR TORTILLAS

2 c. white (wheat) flour
2 T. fresh lard
1 tsp. salt
1/2 c. warm water

Sift flour and salt into a bowl. Pure lard gives the best texture and flavor and it should be creamed, or mixed by hand, to the consistency of face cream. No mixers. Tortillas are made by hand. Work flour and salt with lard and mix well. Add warm water to make a soft dough. Flour varies; you may need more water. Knead dough until springy in a bowl or on a board. Divide dough into balls about the size of small eggs. Cover and allow to rest 10 to 20 minutes (one of the secrets of tender tortillas).

Pat thin with hands or roll thin with rolling pin. Bake, ungreased, on both sides, until freckled with brown. Heat should be medium-hot, as for pancakes, not hot-hot. If tortillas puff up, press down lightly with a clean towel. Recipe makes about a dozen 6-7 inch tortillas. Store any that are not wolfed down in a plastic bag and refrigerate or freeze.

QUICK STYLE FRIJOLES REFRITOS
" REFRIED BEANS"

1 c. bacon drippings (preferrably), vegetable oil or lard
1 recipe of pinto beans

Heat bacon drippings over medium heat in heavy skillet. Add 1/4 of the beans at a time and mash with fork or potato masher. Continue to mash until well-blended. Beans should be shiny. Overcooking causes dryness. Serve as a dip with tortilla chips or as an accompaniment to many other dishes.

OUTLAW BEEF BURRITOS

1 med. onion, finely chopped
1/2 green bell pepper, grated
2 T. oil
2 lbs. lean ground beef
2 tsp. chili powder
1 tsp. ground cumin
2 dashes Tabasco sauce
2 dashes Worcestershire sauce
1 8-oz can red kidney beans, drained
1 8-oz. can tomato sauce
Salt and freshly ground pepper
12 flour tortillas
2 lbs. Monterey Jack cheese, grated
1 4-oz. can green chilies, cut in strips

Saute onions and bell pepper in oil in heavy skillet for 3 minutes. Add ground beef and brown, adding chili powder, cumin, Tabasco, Worcestershire sauce, kidney beans, tomato sauce and salt and pepper to taste. Cover and cook over low heat for 30 minutes. Heat each tortilla in dry, hot iron skillet until it begins to puff. Remove to plate or board. Put a large spoonful of the filling in the center and sprinkle with grated cheese and green chili strips. Fold the side edges into the middle and roll up. Serve immediately. Yield: 12 burritos

TACO SALAD

1 head lettuce, rinsed, well drained, chopped and chilled
2-3 lg. tomatoes, rinsed, chopped and chilled
1 1/2-2 c. American cheese, shredded (keep refrigerated)
*1 lb. hamburger (cooked and drained)
*2 c. pinto beans, cooked and drained
*1 bottle Catalina dressing
1 15-oz. bag reg. Fritos

In a large bowl toss together lettuce and tomatoes; set aside. In a separate bowl stir together meat, beans and dressing. Pour meat mixture and cheese into salad; toss lightly. To serve, add Fritos and enjoy.
*These items should be at room temperature.

QUESO TORTILLAS

1 lb. white melting cheese such as Monterey Jack, mozzarella or Havarti
3 T. oil
1 lg. yellow onion, chopped
1/2 c. sweet bell pepper, chopped
1 lb. mushrooms, sliced
1/2 c. heavy cream
Flour tortillas

Grate the cheese and place it in a large, shallow oven-proof dish. You may use any white cheese that melts and becomes stringy or you may use a combination of those suggested above. Place the cheese in a preheated 200 degree oven to slowly melt for 10 minutes or until it is allowed to become rubbery. Meanwhile, heat the oil in a large frying pan. When hot, saute the onions and bell pepper for 3 to 4 minutes over a moderate flame. Stir in the sliced mushrooms and continue cooking over a high flame for 45 minutes or until they become moist looking and darken slightly in color. Remove the cheese from the oven. It should look three-quarters melted. Gradually stir in the cream. Add the saute mixture little by little including the liquid remaining in the pan until all ingredients are thoroughly blended. Serve immediately by spreading on hot, fresh flour tortillas.

SOUTH OF THE BORDER SALAD

1/2 lb. ground beef, browned in skillet and drained
1/2 head lettuce, torn into small pieces
1 tomato, chopped
1/2 c. Cheddar cheese, grated
1 c. reg. Fritos
1/2 c. Catalina dressing

Toss first five ingredients and just before serving, add the Fritos and dressing. Serves 3-4.

INDIAN

APACHE ACORN STEW

2 1/2-3 lbs. round steak
Sweet acorns (enough to make 3/4 c. of acorn flour
Salt
Wooden or plastic bowl

Cut the round steak into small bite-size pieces and cook in about one quart of water. Let it simmer for about three hours or until meat is well done. Salt to taste. Shell the sweet acorns and grind them into very fine flour until you have about 3/4 cup of flour. Strain the broth from the meat (it will be used later). Shred the meat and placing it in a wooden or plastic bowl, mix it with the acorn flour (aluminum discolors the flour). Pour the hot broth over this mixture and stir. It is now ready to serve in individual bowls. Often times fried bread is served with this stew. Makes 6 servings.

APACHE CHARCOAL-BROILED BUFFALO STEAKS

Buffal Steaks (unfrozen) 1" thick
Salt and pepper
Other spices and seasonings to taste

Broil the steaks on a grill or in a broiling rack about 3 inches from red coals as you would a beef steak. Season with salt and pepper and add your favorite meat sauce.

APACHE FRIED RABBIT (WILD)

Dress swamp or cotton-tail rabbit. Wash, cut up, cover with water. Cook until about done. Take pieces out of liquid, dust with flour, salt and fry brown in a skillet of pork-fat. Makes 4 servings.

APACHE SQUIRREL STEW

Salt and pepper squirrel to taste. Boil in water until very, very tender. Debone. Take 1/2 cup of cooled liquid in which the squirrel was cooked and make dumplings with self-rising flour. Put deboned squirrel back in broth and add cut strips of dumplings to broth and squirrel while cooking. Add a little butter; and if you wish, you may drop three or four eggs into this mixture. Do not stir until eggs are done. (You may add about 1/2 cup of sweet milk to the dumplings before adding eggs, if you wish.)

HOPI BAKED SWEET POTATOES AND HICKORY NUT SAUCE

1 c. hickory nuts
3 c. water
6-8 baking sweet potatoes
Sugar to taste

Prepare hickory nuts a day ahead of time as follows: Beat 1 cup nut meat until it forms butter as in peanut butter. Roll in a ball and place in refrigerator. The next day bake 6 or 8 baking potatoes until done. Peel off skins and place in serving bowl. Pour about 3 cups scalding water over ball and stir until it has completely melted. Add enough sugar to taste and pour over sweet potatoes and serve. Makes 4 servings.

HOPI INDIAN CORN

1 can whole kernel corn
1 sm. pkg. black walnuts
1/2 tsp. black walnut flavoring
2 T. butter

Empty a can of corn packed in water (not creamed corn) into a pot. Add sufficient water and heat, also adding a small package of black walnuts. Then add about 1/2 teaspoon of black walnut flavoring which is available at most grocery stores. Heat with 2 tablespoon butter and serve.

HOPI LAMB STEW

2 lbs. young lamb, cut in chunks
Water to cover
Nanakopsie, if available, a handful
6-8 cups hominy
1 dried red chili pepper, crushed fine
Salt

Remove fat from lamb and cut in bite size pieces. Put in pot and cover with water. Bring to a boil and scoop off any scum. Add nanakopsie, crushed red pepper and salt. Reduce heat, cover and simmer 2 hours or more. Add hominy and cook over low heat all day, until kernels are skin bursting tender. Serve in bowls with pieces of adobe bread for mopping the broth.

INDIAN CHARLIE'S INDIAN PUDDING

4 c. milk, scalded
2/3 c. yellow cornmeal
1 stick butter
1 c. molasses
1/3 c. sugar
2 eggs, beaten slightly
2 tsp. cinnamon
2 tsp. ground ginger
1 tsp. nutmeg
1/8 tsp. salt
2 tsp. vanilla
1 1/2 c. cold milk

In the top of a double boiler, combine the scalded milk and cornmeal. Cook over rapidly boiling water for 30 minutes, stirring constantly. Stir in butter until melted. Stir in molasses, sugar, spices, salt and vanilla. Mix 1/2 cup of cold milk with the eggs before stirring eggs into mixture. Pour mixture into buttered 2 quart casserole dish. Pour remaining cup of cold milk into casserole, but do not stir.

Set casserole dish in a pan of boiling water in oven. (you may set casserole in empty pan and pour boiling water into pan for greater convenience.) Water in pan should reach half-way up side of casserole dish. Bake uncovered in slow (300 degree) oven 2 1/2 to 3 hours. Serve warm with cream.

*Apache Reservation, Globe, Arizona, 1941

INDIAN CHESTNUT BREAD

Peel one pound of nuts and scald to take off the inside skin. Add enough cornmeal to hold nuts together, mixing nuts and cornmeal with boiling water. Wrap in green fodder or green corn shucks, tying each bun securely with white twine. Place in a pot of boiling water and cook until done. Salt when eating, if desired. Bean bread can be made the same way but cook the beans until tender before adding cornmeal. No salt should be added before or during cooking or the bread will crumble. Makes 5-6 servings.

INDIAN PUDDING

1/4 c. cornmeal
2 c. hot milk
1/4 c. sugar
1/8 tsp. baking soda
1/2 tsp. salt
1/2 tsp. ground ginger
1/2 tsp. ground cinnamon
1/4 c. molasses
1 c. cold milk
Whipped cream
Nutmeg

Stir cornmeal, a little at a time, into the hot milk and cook in the top of a double boiler, stirring constantly, for 15 minutes or until thick. Remove from heat. Mix together sugar, baking soda, salt, ginger and cinnamon, then stir into the cornmeal mixture. Add molasses and cold milk, mixing thoroughly. Pour into a one quart casserole dish and bake in a preheated 275 degree oven for 2 hours. Serve warm with whipped cream and a light sprinkling of freshly-grated nutmeg.

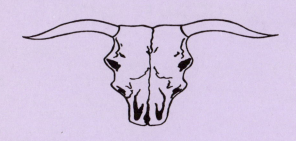

NAVAJO PEANUT SOUP

1 9 1/4 oz. jar dry roasted peanuts
2 c. water
2 c. milk
2 5.4 gram pkgs. instant chicken broth
1 T. minced chives

Chop the nuts fine and puree in a blender. Place the nuts and the remaining ingredients in a large saucepan, and heat, stirring for 5 to 20 minutes. Serve hot. Make the portions small—the soup is rich. Makes 6 servings.

NAVAJO YAM CAKES

2 c. sifted flour
1 1/2 tsp. sugar
1 1/2 tsp. salt
2 1/2 tsp. baking powder
1/2 c. salad oil
1/2 c. milk
1 cup mashed yams or sweet potaotes

Sift flour, baking powder, sugar and salt into a bowl. Pour oil and milk into a measuring cup but do not stir. Add to yams. Blend well. Add to flour mixture and mix lightly with a fork until mixture holds together. Turn dough out onto a floured surface and knead gently until smooth, about 12 kneading strokes. Roll dough about 1/4-inch thick and cut into rounds with floured biscuit cutter. Place rounds on a baking sheet. Bake at 425 degrees for 10-20 minutes. Serve hot or split when cold and toast. Makes 18 3-inch cakes.

PAPAGO BAKED PUMPKIN

1 sm. pumpkin
2 T. apple cider
2 T. honey
2 T. melted butter or margarine

Wash the pumpkin well, place on a pie pan, and bake in a moderate oven, 350 degrees, for 1 1/2 hours. Remove from the oven and cut a hole in the top of the pumpkin about 3 to 4-inches in diameter. Scoop out pulp and seeds. Mix together the honey, cider, and melted butter or margarine. Baste the mixture over the flesh of the pumpkin. Replace top, return to moderate oven and continue to bake for 35 to 40 minutes longer, basting occasionally. Serve whole, scooping out the individual portions at the table or cut into wedges as you would a melon. Ladle a little of the cider mixture over each serving. Makes 6-8 servings.

PIMA CACTUS SALAD

1 7 1/4 oz. can natural cactus in salt water, drained
1 7 oz. can pimiento, drained
Dressing:
3 T. salad oil
1 scallion, washed and minced
1 clove garlic, peeled and crushed
2 T. tarragon vinegar
1/8 tsp. fresh ground pepper

Arrange a bed of cactus on a small platter. Slice the pimiento into julienne strips and place over the cactus. Mix together the dressing ingredients and pour over salad. Marinate in the refrigerator one hour before serving. Makes 4 servings.

PIMA CRISPY FRIED FISH

2 lb. sm. dressed fish
1 1/2 tsp. salt
Dash pepper
Fat or oil for frying
1/4 c. milk
1/2 c. flour
1/4 c. cornmeal

Thaw frozen fish, clean, wash and dry fish. Add salt and pepper to milk. Mix flour and cornmeal. Dip fish in milk and roll in flour mixture. Fry in hot fat at moderate heat for 4 to 5 minutes or until brown on one side. Turn carefully and fry 4 to 5 minutes longer until other side is brown and fish flakes easily when tested with a fork. Drain on paper. Makes 4-6 servings.

PIMA FRY BREAD

Oil
Flour
1/2 c. yellow cornmeal
2 T. baking powder
1 T. sugar
1 tsp. salt
1 T. shortening
2 c. buttermilk

Pour oil into deep fryer and heat to 350 degrees. Mix 2 1/2 cups flour and remaining dry ingredients. Cut in shortening with fingertips. Add buttermilk to make a fairly thick dough.

Place on floured surface and knead well, adding flour, until thick and pliable. Place in oiled bowl and let stand 30 minutes. Break off handfuls and flatten and stretch dough (with oiled hands) to saucer size. Prick the center with a knife.

Drop into deep, hot fat and fry until golden brown, about 1 minute per side. Turn once. Drain.

PIMA HUCKLEBERRY BREAD

2 c. self-rising flour
1 c. sugar
1 c. milk
2 c. berries (huckleberries or blueberries)
1 egg
1 stick butter
1 tsp. vanilla extract

Cream egg, butter and sugar together. Add flour, milk and vanilla. Sprinkle flour on berries to prevent them from going to the bottom. Add berries to mixture. Put in baking pan and bake in oven at 350 degrees approximately 40 minutes or until done.

PIMA FRY BREAD

3 c. flour
1 T. shortening, lard or corn oil
3/4 c. warm water
3 tsp. baking powder
1 tsp. salt

Measure dry ingredients into deep mixing bowl. Add shortening and knead with hands until dough is in small pea-sized pieces. Add warm, not hot, water and knead with hands until dough is smooth and leaves sides of bowl. Knead at least 5 minutes. Cover with clean dish cloth, place in warm place to rise for 30 minutes. The secret for tender, light Fry Bread, is in the kneading and resting. Divide dough into portions about golf-ball size and pat, slap or roll out as round as possible, 1/4-inch thick. Fry in hot shortening or oil about 1-inch in depth. Fry both sides until light golden, not dark brown. Top with refried beans, powdered sugar or honey.

A Navajo Taco is Fry Bread of generous proportions, heaped with beans, grated cheese, chopped lettuce, tomato and onion and jolts of fired-up salsa.

PIMA FRIED HOMINY

6 strips bacon cut into pieces
1/8 tsp. pepper
1/2 tsp. salt
2 lbs. drained hominy
2 scallions sliced thin
  (include tops)

Fry the bacon in a large, heavy skillet until brown and crisp. Stir in hominy and salt, stirring for 5 minutes. Add pepper and scallions, stirring for 5 minutes more. Makes 6-8 servings.

PIMA FRY BREAD

4 T. honey
3 T. oil
1 T. salt
2 c. hot water
1 T. (1 pkg.) active dry yeast
3 c. unbleached white flour
2 tsp. baking powder
2 to 4 c. additional flour

(Start the dough mixture about 2 to 2 1/2 hours before serving.)

Mix together the honey, oil and salt. Stir in the hot water. Mix well. Sprinkle the yeast on top of mixture.

Cover with a cloth and allow to stand about 10 minutes or until yeast bubbles. Add flour and baking powder. Stir well.

Add more flour until mixture is firm and cleans the hands. Use from 2 to 4 cups flour for this step. Place in a greased bowl. Turn over to grease top. Cover and allow to rise until double (about an hour). Punch down and divide in half, then each half in 8 parts. Form each piece into a ball and permit to rise until ready to cook.

Heat deep fat to frying temperature. Take ball of dough and flatten with hands, using stretching action. When dough is very thin and about 6-8 inches in diameter, drop into hot fat and cook until golden (about 1 1/2 minutes each side.) Drain on paper toweling and serve hot with honey or powdered sugar.

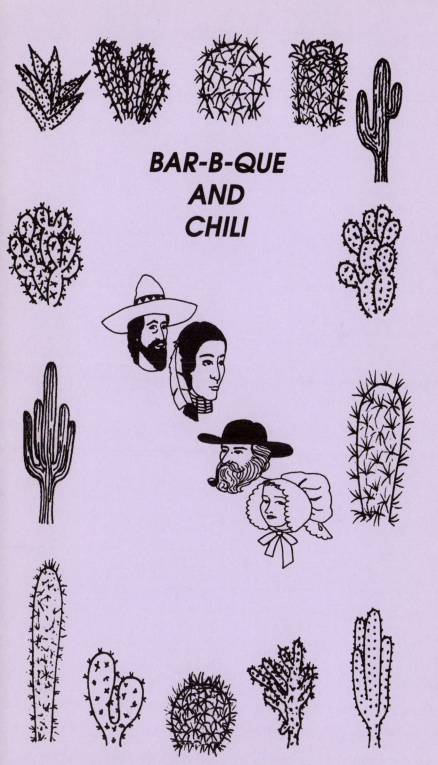

BAR-B-Q AND CHILI

BAR-B-Q

GRAND CANYON BARBECUE SAUCE

1 c. butter
1/4 c. vinegar
1 T. sugar
2 1/4 tsp. chili powder
1 1/2 tsp. Worcestershire sauce
1/4 tsp. pepper
1 T. minced onion
2 1/2 c. consome or beef stock
1 1/4 tsp. dry mustard
2 tsp. salt
Dash cayenne pepper
1/2 tsp. Tabasco
1 T. paprika
1 garlic clove

Combine all ingredients; boil 20 minutes. Remove garlic clove. Use to baste pork, beef or chicken as it boils. Makes about 3 cups sauce.

To baste, tie a clean cloth on the end of a long stick; dip the cloth in the sauce and then rub it on the meat. Do this constantly. When having a picnic, several "swabbers" can "spell" one another and make it easier.

A crew of "turners" can be chosen. You will need a fork tied to the end of a long stick. Keep turning the meat so it will be evenly broiled.

BARBECUED CHICKEN

Prepare a whole chicken, preferably 2 1/2 pounds, not over 3 pounds in weight. Sprinkle the inside of the chicken with a little celery salt and fill it with quartered chunks of onion and 1-inch chunks of celery. Sew up the chicken, truss the back and tie up the wings and legs so that the chicken can be handled easily without the legs and wings protruding too far. Cook in a regular closed barbecue oven on a very slow fire for 2 1/2 to 3 hours, basting every 10-15 minutes with baste made up of a can of consomme, 1/2 pound melted butter, juice of 2 lemons. When chicken is done, it should be tender, moist and nicely browned. Split chick in half with a pair of game sheers; remove the onion and celery and serve 1/2 chicken to a person.

BEST IN THE WEST BAR B Q RIBS

Ribs and Cooking Liquid
4 qts. beef broth
3/4 c. red wine vinegar
1 T. Paprika
1 T. cayenne pepper
1 1/2 T. Tabasco sauce
1 1/2 T. ground cumin
1 1/2 T. garlic powder
1 T. ground ginger
1 c. tomato paste
1/4 c. honey
1 T. salt
4 slabs baby-back ribs
 (1 1/4 lbs. each)

SPICE MIXTURE
1/4 c. garlic salt
1 T. ground white pepper
1/2 c. paprika
1/4 c. dry mustard
1/4 c. red wine vinegar
1/4 c. Worcestershire sauce
1/2 c. beer

BARBECUE SAUCE
1 c. chili sauce
1 c. catsup
1/4 c. steak sauce
1/4 c. Worcestershire sauce
1 T. finely pressed garlic
2 T. prepared horseradish
3 T. dry mustard
1 T. Tabasco sauce
1 T. molasses
1 T. jalapeno salsa
1 T. red wine vinegar

(You may buy boullion cubes at your local grocer's and this will be adequate for broth.) Combine all cooking liquid ingredients in a large pot; stir well. Bring to a simmer over medium heat. Add ribs and simmer until tender but not falling apart, about 1 hour and 45 minutes. When done, carefully transfer ribs to a cookie sheet. Reserve liquid for future use, if desired.

Combine all Spice Mixture ingredients in a medium-sized bowl to form a paste (add more beer if too dry). Rub paste over all surfaces of ribs. Refrigerate until ready to cook. (Can be prepared in advance.)

Combine Barbecue Sauce ingredients in a medium-sized bowl. Whisk until well blended. Adjust seasoning to taste. Preheat oven to 400 degrees. Cover a cookie sheet with foil. Place ribs on foil and coat with 2 cups Barbecue Sauce. Cover entire sheet with foil and bake on center rack of oven for 10 minutes. Unwrap ribs and place on a grill (or under broiler) to char. Serve at once with the remaining Barbecue Sauce. Serves 4 hungry people.

HOLBROOK BARBECUE BEEF OR PORK RIBS

5 lbs. beef or pork ribs
3 c. Ace High Barbecue Sauce

Place ribs in a flat pan or dish. Pour sauce over ribs, turning so as to coat both sides; pierce meat with a large fork. Marinate 8 hours, turning once. Remove ribs from marinade and brush off excess sauce to avoid burning. Broil or cook over coals for 10 minutes. Brush with marinade and cook 4 to 5 minutes more. Heat remaining sauce and serve with ribs. (Ribs may be cooked in a covered pan in a 350 degree oven for 1 1/2 hours, if desired.) Makes 4-6 servings.

ACE HIGH BARBECUE SAUCE

1 c. strong black coffee
1 c. Worcestershsire sauce
1 c. catsup
1/2 c. cider vinegar
1/2 c. brown sugar
3 T. chili powder
2 tsp. salt
2 c. chopped onions
1/4 c. minced hot chili peppers
6 cloves garlic, minced

Combine all ingredients in a saucepan and simmer 25 minutes. Strain or puree in a blender or food processor. Refrigerate between uses. Makes 5 cups.

2-C RANCH BARBECUE SAUCE

2 14-oz. bottles catsup
1 12-oz. bottle chili sauce
1 T. dry mustard
1/3 c. prepared mustard
2 T. fresh ground pepper
1 1/2 c. wine vinegar
1 c. fresh lemon juice
1/4 c. Worcestershire sauce
1 1/2 c. brown sugar
1/2 c. bottles steak sauce
Dash Tabasco sauce
1 T. soy sauce
2 T. cooking oil
1 12-oz. can beer
Minced or crushed garlic

Combine all ingredients. Stores for several weeks in refrigerator. May be frozen. Good with chicken or any meat. Excellent as marinade. Makes 6 pints.

MUSTARD DIP

1/2 c. sugar
4 tsp. dry mustard
1 tsp. salt
2 eggs, beaten
1/2 c. milk
1/2 c. vinegar
1/4 c. butter

In the top of double boiler, stir sugar, mustard and salt. Separately whisk eggs and milk. Whisk into dry mixture. Add vinegar and butter. Cook in double boiler for 15 minutes, stirring frequently. Mixture will thicken some. Serve with ham or chicken.

ARIZONA'S FAVORITE BARBECUE SAUCE

2 med. onions, sliced
2 sticks, margarine
1 6-oz. jar mustard
1 15-oz. bottle cooking oil
1 16-oz. bottle red vinegar
4 lemons, thinly sliced
1 6-oz. bottle Worcestershire sauce
2 tsp. Louisiana hot sauce
1 12-oz. can of beer
1 c. brown sugar
1 5-oz bottle Heinz "57" sauce, optional
2 tsp. Lawry's seasoned salt
2 tsp. black pepper

"Flip" is famous at State County Agent meetings for his fine barbecue and this is his special sauce.

In a large, heavy saucepan, saute onions in the margarine. Add all ingredients except mustard, Heinz "57" sauce and brown sugar. Simmer another 20 minutes. Do not get too hot, it will destroy spiceiness. Use to baste any meat!

HOT AND SPICY BBQ SAUCE

1 pod garlic
5 med. onions, chopped
1 c. Wesson oil
2 bottles catsup
1/3 c. Louisiana sauce
2/3 c. Worcestershire sauce
2 c. vinegar
Fifth of sherry, if desired

Brown onions and garlic in small amount of oil. Add catsup, hot sauce, Worcestershire sauce, vinegar and the rest of the oil. Blend well over slow fire. Remove from heat and add sherry. Mix well. May be refrigerated and used over and over.

DRY BBQ SAUCE

2 heaping T. black pepper
6 heaping T. salt
1 1/2 heaping T. garlic powder
1 heaping T. red pepper
3 heaping T. chili powder
4 heaping T. paprika

Mix all ingredients together in bowl. Before barbecuing chicken, ribs, briskets, fish or pork chops, sprinkle on very heavy. This mixture serves as a "dry" barbecue sauce but makes a crust, sealing in juices.

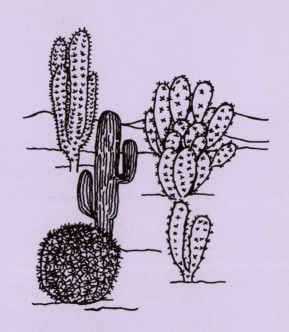

BLACK JACK BBQ SAUCE

1 c. strong black coffee
1 c. Worcestershire sauce
1 c. catsup
1/2 c. cider vinegar
1/2 c. brown sugar
3 T. chili powder
2 tsp. salt
2 c. onions, chopped
1/4 c. minced hot chili peppers
6 cloves garlic, minced

Combine all ingredients in a saucepan and simmer 25 minutes. Strain or puree in a blender or food processor. Refrigerate between uses. Makes 5 cups.

ORIGINAL HOT SAUCE OR BARBECUE SAUCE

This sauce was brought over here by the Spanish into Mexico in the 17th Century. This is the only original hot bar-b-q sauce. This is what you need:

1/3 to 1/2 c. ground red pepper (depending on taste)
1/4 c. all-purpose flour
1/4 tsp. garlic powder
1 tsp. sugar
1/4 tsp. salt
3/4 c. cider vinegar
3/4 c. water

Mix up the dry ingredients first. Pour in the vinegar and water. Stir it all up real good until it's smooth. Put it all in a saucepan. Put over low heat and simmer it along for about 6-7 minutes until it thickens up—like you like it. All this will cook down to about 1 pint of good eating. Pour it up into something you can keep covered in the refrigerator.

NOTE: If this sauce is too hot, you can add 1 cup brown sugar or 1 cup molasses to suit your taste.

BARBECUE SALT

1 lb. brown sugar
1 c. salt
1 1/2 oz. paprika
2 T. black pepper
1 1/2 tsp. cayenne pepper
1/4 tsp. cinnamon
1 T. garlic powder

Mix all ingredients. Place in sealed container and keep refrigerated. Rub on meat before grilling.

BARBECUED GOAT

1 cabrito (very young goat), cut into pieces
2 lg. onions
8 ozs. bottled Italian dressing
1 bottle barbecue sauce with smoke
2 or 3 cans of beer

Place pieces of goat in a large pan. Chop onions in a blender and mix with lemon juice, vegetable oil and 4 ounces of the dressing. Simmer in a saucepan until onions are cooked. Pour over meat and wrap in foil. Refrigerate and let tenderize 5 hours. Smoke goat in a smoker 3 to 4 hours, basting with a mixture of barbecue sauce, the remainder of the Italian dressing and beer (sauce will be thin). Brown in smoker and serve. Serves 6.

ARIZONA'S BEST STEW OR BBQ

This recipe was given to me by a black woman near Yuma, AZ about 1961. Talk about BBQ, this is probably the only true BBQ that has no preservatives or additives added to it. I used to cook this for the boys at rodeos, saloons and different places. Guaranteed the best BBQ, stew or whatever-you-want-to-call-it, you'll ever eat!

To simplify, use a pressure cooker. Using your pressure cooker's instructions, cook:

3 lbs. pork, preferably pork loin
3 lbs. beef
3 lbs. chicken

VERY IMPORTANT-SAVE THE BROTH. After the meat is cooked, run through a grinder or cut real fine with a knife. Then put meat back into the broth. Add 1 to 2 cups of your favorite hot sauce, depending on your taste. Add 1/4 cup smoked liquid and/or 1 quart bottled, smoked BBQ sauce. Cook for approximately 4 hours on real low heat.

*God bless the black lady who gave me this recipe, as it sure has made a lot of people happy!

BARBECUED PORK OR BEEF ROAST

1 eye-of-round or pork roast (4-5 lbs.)
1/2 tsp. salt
1/2 tsp. pepper
1/2 tsp. garlic salt
1/2 tsp. meat tenderizer
1 c. water
3/4 c. peeled, chopped tomato
1/4 c. vinegar
1/4 c. catsup
2 T. chopped onion
1 clove garlic, minced
2 stalks celery, sliced
1 T. Worcestershire sauce
1 tsp. lemon juice
1/4 c. butter or margarine
1 c. barbecue sauce

Rub roast on all sides with salt, pepper, garlic salt and meat tenderizer; place roast in a 13X9X2" baking pan. Set aside. Combine next 9 ingredients in a large saucepan. Bring to a boil. Reduce heat and simmer 15 minutes. Stir butter and barbecue sauce into liquid.

*Tucson City Stockyard, Tucson, AZ, 1959.

PIONEER MUSTARD SHORT RIBS

4 lbs. beef short ribs, cut into pieces
1/3 c. prepared mustard
2 T. lemon juice
2 cloves garlic, crushed
1 T. sugar
1 tsp. salt
1/2 tsp. pepper
4 med. onions, sliced
1/4 c. shortening

Place meat in shallow glass dish. Mix mustard, lemon juice, garlic, sugar, salt and pepper; spread on meat. Top with onions. Cover tightly; refrigerate for 24 hours, turning occasionally. Brown ribs in shortening over medium heat; pour off drippings. Add onions and pour marinade over meat. Cover tightly; cook in 350 degree oven for 2 hours.

WITTENBURG BEEF KABOBS

Bacon strips
1 1/2 lbs. sirloin tip
 cut into 1/2" cubes
1/2 c. peanut oil
1/2 c. wine vinegar
1/2 c. onion, finely chopped
2 T. Worcestershire sauce
1 tsp. dried basil, crushed
1 tsp. dried rosemary, crushed
1/2 tsp. pepper
1/4 tsp. bottled hot
 pepper sauce
Green pepper wedges
Cherry tomatoes
Onion wedges
Mushroom caps
Zucchini slices
Summer squash slices

Place beef cubes in a bowl or plastic bag. Mix peanut oil, wine vinegar, onion, Worcestershire sauce, basil, rosemary, pepper and hot pepper sauce. Pour over meat coating all sides. Cover and marinate in refrigerator 4-6 hours or overnight. Remove beef cubes from marinade, reserving the marinade for basting. If beef is exceptionally lean, wrap with small strips of bacon. Skewer steak alternating with vegetables. Grill or broil until done, approximately 12-15 minutes, turning and basting frequently with remaining marinade until meat is browned and vegetables are tender. Serves 4. The secret to successful beef kabobs is to have everything finished cooking at the same time. Many raw vegetables take longer than the meat. Charbroil them before cooking with kabobs or cook on separate skewers a longer amount of time and combine with meat when serving.

BARBECUE SLAW

1 sm. head lettuce
2 stalks celery
1 med. green pepper
1 med. onion
3/4 c. catsup
1/4 c. vinegar
2 T. sugar
1 T. Worcestershire sauce
1 T. prepared mustard
1 tsp. salt
Dash cayenne pepper

Grate, chop or grind cabbage, celery, green pepper and onion. Combine catsup and remaining ingredients. Mix with vegetables. Chill several hours.

BULL RIDERS' SLAW

3 c. green cabbage, firmly packed and thinly shredded
2 T. minced onion
1/4 c. sugar
3/4 tsp. salt
1/4 tsp. dry mustard
1/4 tsp. celery seed
1/4 c. white vinegar
1/4 c. salad oil

Sprinkle cabbage with onion and sugar. In small saucepan, whisk together the remaining ingredients, stirring often. Bring to a boil and put over the cabbage; mix thoroughly. Cover and chill at least 4 hours or overnight. Keeps well for 5 days. For color, sprinkle slivered green peppers on top of slaw at serving time.

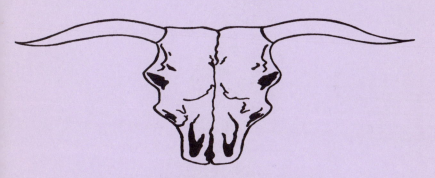

TOMBSTONE HOT BEANS
(Crockpot)

Soak:
2 lbs. beans overnight, pour off water
1 tall Coke
2 tsp. ground mustard
2 T. mineral oil
Water (more than enough to cover beans)
1/2 lb. salt pork
6 cloves garlic
2 lg. onions
Hot peppers, as desired, chopped
2 or 3 cans tomato sauce
2 tsp. salt

First hour add to drained beans: Coke, ground mustard, mineral oil and water. Second hour, add: Salt pork. Third hour, add: 6 cloves garlic. Fourth hour, add: Onions and hot peppers and fifth hour, add: Tomato sauce and salt.

Simmer until beans thicken; in all, cook at least 5 hours.

RESTAURANT SALSA

3 med. size fresh tomatoes, finely chopped
1/2 med. size white onion, finely chjopped
8 green onions, finely chopped
2 T. fresh cilantro, finely chopped
3 jalapenos, seeded and finely chopped
1/4 c. lime juice
2 oz. white tequila

Mix all ingredients and refrigerate at least two hours before serving. Makes approximately 1 cup.

REAL HOT TACO SAUCE

3 sm. cans tomato paste
4 tsp. chilitipins (crushed dry red peppers)
1/4 c. white vinegar
1 tsp. salt
1 tsp. garlic powder
Pinch of oregano

Combine ingredients and mix. Add water as is needed. This recipe makes about one pint of hot sauce.

TRAIL BOSS SALSA

5 lg. fresh ripe red tomatoes, coarsely chopped
2 tomatillos, coarsely chopped
1 lg. white onion, finely chopped
4 oz. chopped green chili
1 clove peeled garlic, run through a garlic press
3 T. olive oil
3 T. red wine vinegar
2 tsp. minced fresh cilantro
1/2 tsp. garlic salt
1/2 tsp. ground black pepper
1/4 tsp. ground oregano

Mix all ingredients together and chill. Serve with tortilla chips or as a side dish with meat. Makes approximately 2 cups.

QUICK GREEN CHILI SALSA

10 good-size roasted green chilies
1 green tomato
1/2 tsp. garlic salt
2 tsp. fresh cilantro

Peel chilies, remove stems and seeds. Peel tomato and chop in a blender. Add chili, garlic salt and cilantro to tomato and blend. Makes approximately one cup.

CHILI

PECOS BILL'S WORLD CHAMPIONSHIP CHILI RECIPE

10 T. bacon grease
6 T. olive oil
3 med. onions, chopped
3 med. green peppers, chopped
4 sm. cloves garlic
2 lg. stalks celery, chopped
1/2 or more fresh jalepeno pepper, diced
1/2 tsp. sage
8 lbs. sausage, coarse ground
1 7-oz. can diced green chilies
2 14 1/2 oz. cans stewed tomatoes
1 15-oz. can tomato sauce
1 6-oz. can tomato paste
6 oz. chili powder
3 T. cumnin
Tabasco to taste
1 12-oz. can beer
1 bottle mineral water
3 bay leaves
1 T. sugar
2 tsp. salt
Garlic salt to taste
1 tsp. oregano
3 tsp. parsley flakes
1 tsp. black pepper
1 T. paprika

(If available, I use 1 cup of Mr. & Mrs. "T" Bloody Mary Mix).

Brown sausage in bacon grease and olive oil in large pot. Add green pepper, onion, celery in pan and saute. Drain oil, then add rest of ingredients and cook slowly for three hours on low heat. Stir often. Makes 24 servings. Championship chili does not require beans, but most restaurants do prefer to add beans as a filler.

After chili is cooked you can add 4 to 5 (20 oz.) cans red kidney beans, washed and drained. Add to chili and cook 15 minutes.

SHEEPHERDER'S CHILI

2 lbs. ground lamb
1 c. onions, chopped
3/4 c. green peppers, chopped
2 med. cloves garlic, minced
28 oz. can tomatoes, chopped
1 T. salt
1 bay leaf
1 T. chili powder
2 4-oz. cans Ortega brand diced green chilies
16 oz. can pinto beans, drained

Brown lamb in a large skillet until crumbled. Drain onion, green pepper, and garlic and cook until vegetables are tender. Stir in remaining ingredients except beans. Simmer, covered, for 35 minutes, stirring occasionaly. Remove cover and add beans. Simmer, uncovered, 10 minutes or until desired consistency. Garnish with sour cream or Monterey Jack cheese, if desired. Serves: 6-8.

TRIPLE C CHILI

It's hot, so have plenty of margaritas or buttermilk on hand to help neutralize the burning.

3 lbs. chili ground meat
15 oz. can tomato sauce
1 c. water
1 tsp. Tabasco
3 T. chili powder, heaping
1 T. oregano, heaping
1 T. comino, heaping (seeds or powder)
6 garlic cloves, chopped
1 tsp. salt
1 tsp. cayenne pepper
4 whole tamu mild jalapenos
4 or 5 chilipiquins
2 T. flour, heaping

Sear the meat in a large skillet until grey in color. Put the meat into a chili pot with the tomato sauce and enough water to cover the meat by 1/2 inch. Add the remaining ingredients, except the whole pepper pods and stir. Put in the chili pods and jalapenos whole. Be careful not to break them because they are for flavor. Eating them is left up to the individual. Simmer for one hour and 15 minutes. Skim off excess grease. Add thickener made of 2 heaping tabelspoons flour and water and simmer for additional 30 minutes (or overnight...it can't hurt.)

WILD CARD CHILI

1 lb. chopped beef
1/2 c. chopped onion
1 16-oz. can red beans
1 16 oz. can refried beans
1 8-oz. can tomato sauce
1 c. water
1 tsp. chopped hot red peppers
1/2 tsp. salt
1/2 tsp. garlic salt
1/8 tsp. pepper
1/8 tsp. cayenne
3 T. chili powder
1 T. molasses

Brown beef with onions in a Dutch oven; pour off fat. Add remaining ingredients; cover and simmer 1 hour, stirring occasionaly. Makes 6 servings.

CHILI FIESTA

6 lbs. ground beef
3 c. onions, chopped
2 c. green peppers, chopped
6 garlic cloves, minced
2 28-oz. cans tomatoes, chopped
1 8-oz. can tomato sauce
3 T. salt
2 bay leaves
3 T. chili powder
4 7-oz. cans diced green chilies
3 16-oz. cans pinto beans, drained
2 env. instant beef broth

Brown beef in an 8-quart saucepan until crumbled. Drain. Stir in remaining ingredients. Simmer, uncovered, 1 hour or until desired consistency has been achieved. Garnish with sour cream or Monterey Jack cheese, if desired.
Serves 10 to 12.

CACTUS CHILI
(The Tequila Adds the Needles)

1/2 c. flour
4 tsp. salt
1/4 tsp. pepper
3 lbs. pork shoulder, cut into 1-inch cubes
1/4 c. oil
1/4 c. instant minced onion
1/4 tsp. instant minced garlic
1 c. water
1 16-oz. can tomatoes, chopped
4-oz. tequila
1 1/2 T. chili powder
1 tsp. ground cumin seed, optional
2 16-oz. cans kidney beans, drained
1/2 c. golden raisins

Combine flour, 2 teaspoons salt and pepper in a large bowl. Add pork and toss, coating each piece thoroughly. Shake off excess flour and reserve. Heat oil in a heavy skillet. Brown thoroughly one third of the meat at a time. Combine dried vegetables with water to re-hydrate. Add vegetables to pork drippings and brown. Add tomatoes and tequila; stir well. Add chili powder, cumin and reserve flour to tomatoes, blending well. Bring to a boil. Reduce heat, cover and simmer for 1 hour. Add beans and raisins, simmer for 10 minutes. Serve over steamed rice garnished with sliced avocado and shredded Cheddar cheese, if desired. Serves 6 to 8.

SHEEPHERDER'S CHILI

2 lbs. ground lamb
1 c. onions, chopped
3/4 c. green peppers, chopped
2 med. garlic cloves, minced
1 28-oz. can tomatoes, chopped
1 T. salt
1 bay leaf
1 T. chili powder
2 4-oz. cans Ortega brand diced green chilies
1 16-oz. can pinto beans, drained

Brown lamb in a large skillet until crumbled. Drain. Add onion, green pepper and garlic; cook until vegetables are tender. Stir in remaining ingredients except beans. Simmer, covered, for 35 minutes, stirring occasionally. Remove cover and add beans. Simmer, uncovered, 10 minutes or until desired consistency. Garnish with sour cream or Monterey Jack cheese, if desired.

Serves 6 to 8.

YUMA CHILI

2 tsp. salt
3 lbs. ground beef
7-oz. beer
1 T. soy sauce
2 tsp. pepper
2 tsp. paprika
1/2 tsp. sage
2 tsp. sugar
1 T. cumin powder
4 T. chili powder
1/3 c. cornmeal
3 T. A-1 sauce
1/2 c. vinegar
2 jalapeno peppers, diced
2 16-oz. cans tomatoes, chopped
1 12-oz. can tomato paste
1 1/2 lbs. pork shoulder, cubed
1 T. garlic powder
1 7-oz. can Ortega brand diced green chilies

Brown beef thoroughly. Add beer, salt, pepper, paprika, sage, sugar, cumin and chili powder, blending well. Cover and simmer 2 hours. Add remaining ingredients; cover and simmer over low heat for 3 hours, stirring frequently.

Serves 6 to 8.

ARIZONA COTTON CHOPPER'S CHILI

1/4 lb. salt pork, cut into thin strips
2 lbs. ground chuck
2 med. green peppers, chopped
1 med. onion, chopped
2 16-oz. cans whole tomatoes, chopped
1 16-oz. can kidney beans
4 T. chili powder
1 6-oz. can tomato paste
1 tsp. Tabasco sauce
1 qt. water
Salt and pepper to taste

Cook salt pork and ground chuck together in skillet until ground meat is browned. Set aside.

In large pot, saute green peppers and onions, using a small amount of salt pork grease; stir in tomatoes and kidney beans. Add chili powder, tomato paste, Tabasco and enough water to create desired consistency. Stir in meat (including salt pork strips) and simmer, uncovered, 2 hours, stirring frequently. Salt and pepper to taste.

Serves 6.

FLAGSTAFF HOTTER THAN HELL CHILI

1 lg. onion, chopped
2 T. oil
2 lbs. lean chili meat
1 lg. can tomatoes
2 small cans tomato sauce
1 tsp. sugar
2 tsp. ground comino
2 tsp. paprika
1 lg. garlic clove
1 can beer
2 fresh jalapeno peppers
5 T. chili powder
Salt and cayenne pepper to taste*
2 c. cooked pinto beans, optional
1 T. tequila (at least 150 proof)

*Hotness of chili depends on how much cayenne.

Saute chopped onion in oil. Add chili meat and stir until grey. Add remaining ingredients except for tequila and beans. Cook until thick, about 1 1/2 hours. At this point, if you like beans in your chili, add the two cups cooked pinto beans... but make sure there aren't any Texans around. When ready to serve, put into a large bowl, pour tequila over and light. Chili Flambe` for all you gourmets.

ARIZONA MEX CHILI

3 T. oil
1 1/2 lbs. stew beef, cut into 1/4-inch cubes
1 green pepper, seeded and chopped
1 16-oz. can beef broth
2 7-oz. cans Ortega brand green chile salsa
3 T. chili powder
1/2 tsp. cumin powder

Brown beef with oil in a large skillet. Add vegetables and cook until tender. Add beef broth, chili powder and cumin. Cover and cook at medium heat for 2 hours. Remove cover, simmer longer for desired thickness, stirring often.

Serves 4.

Notes

BREADS AND SWEETS

BREADS & SWEETS

BREADS

ARIZONA BISCUITS ON A STICK

1 1/2 c. flour
3/4 c. oats
1 T. baking powder
1 tsp. salt
1/2 c. shortening
1 c. grated sharp Cheddar cheese
1/2 c. milk

Combine flour, oats, baking powder and salt. Cut in shortening until mixture resembles coarse crumbs. Stir in cheese and milk. Knead gently a few times. Divide dough into 24 equal pieces. Flaten in hands and shape around a stick to form a cylinder. Toast over hot coals for 8-10 minutes, turning frequently. Slide off stick and fill with butter and jam to serve. Makes 2 dozen.

BEEF OR PORK BISCUITS

Designed to use leftover beef or pork. Make a dough of the following:

4 c. flour
1 1/4 tsp. salt
1/3 c. vegetable shortening
3 T. baking powder
1/3 c. butter

1 sm. onion
1 med. green pepper
4 oz. jar pimientos
4 oz. can mushroom pieces

Cut in butter and shortening; add **1 c. milk**. Combine until mixture will hold together and form ball. Cover and chill for 2 hours. Grind the roast (approximately 4 cups.)

Mix meat and vegetables; mix into dough. Flour hands and shape mixture into 1-inch balls. Place on greased baking sheets. Indent center of each with thumb (may have to be repeated halfway through baking). Bake approximately 15 minutes or until slightly browned. Serve warm with butter, cheese spread or pepper jelly in indentation. Makes 8-12 dozen.

*BB Ranch, Arizona, 1878, Joe Cook

CORNMEAL BISCUITS

1 1/2 c. all-purpose flour
2 1/2 tsp. baking powder
1/2 tsp. salt
1/2 c. yellow cornmeal
1/3 c. shortening
2/3 c. milk

Sift flour, baking powder and salt into mixing bowl. Blend in cornmeal and shortening, then add milk all at once.

Stir lightly with fork, just enough to moisten all the flour. Knead gently, about 1/2 minute on lightly floured board. Roll dough 3/4-inch thick. Cut with 2-inch cutter and place on lightly greased baking sheet. Bake at 450 degrees 12-15 minutes. Makes 12 biscuits.

OLD STYLE BAKING POWDER BISCUITS

2 c. flour
1/2 tsp. salt
2/3 c. milk
4 tsp. baking powder
4 T. lard

Sift dry ingredients. Cut in fat with knife; slowly add milk. Roll out on a floured board; roll 1/2 to 1-inch thick. Cut biscuits with cutter. Bake at 425 degrees 12-14 minutes. For best results, have ingredients cold and mix lightly.

*This recipe is probably the old standard used by trail cooks, bunkhouse cooks, etc. This recipe could be varied by using buttermilk instead of sweet milk or adding to it onions, bacon bits or even cheese. Some people can make good biscuits and some can't. For instance, if your oven is too hot and you cook them too fast, they're going to be too hard or if your oven is too low and you cook them too slowly, they will be too soggy. Baking biscuits is an art of its own.

CORN BREAD STUFFING

3 c. stale corn bread, crumbled
3 c. stale white bread, crumbled
1/2 lb. butter
2 onions, chopped
3 stalks celery, chopped
1 apple, cored, peeled and chopped
3 sprigs parsley, minced
1 bay leaf, crumbled
1 tsp. dried thyme
1 tsp. dried sage
2 cloves garlic, crushed
Salt and pepper, to taste
Giblets of turkey or 1/2 lb. sausage meat

Crumble breads into large bowl. Chop giblets (or sausage meat) and cook with vegetables in part of the butter until lightly browned. Melt rest of butter and add with the vegetables, apple, herbs and seasonings to the bread. Stir to blend well and stuff into the bird just before roasting.

This is also good old-time stuffing that could be used in turkeys, chickens, pork chops, roast pigs, wild game, etc.

PAPPY'S SKILLET CORN BREAD

3/4 c. flour
1 1/4 c. cormeal
2 tsp. baking powder
1 1/2 T. brown sugar
1 tsp. salt
1 egg, beaten
1 c. milk
3 T. melted butter

Heat a 10-inch cast-iron skillet and melt the 3 tablespoon butter until skillet is sizzling hot. In a mixing bowl, combine dry ingredients. Stir in egg mixed with milk. Add melted butter from skillet. Mix until all ingredients are moistened. Do not overmix. Spread mixture evenly in the hot skillet. Cover with lid. Cook over hot fire (400 degrees on your stove-top thermometer) 30 minutes or until crusty golden brown.

*Arizona, date unknown

POOR CHARLIE'S SOURDOUGH CORN BREAD

1 c. starter (see below)
Cornmeal (enough to make batter)
1 1/2 c. milk
2 T. sugar
2 eggs, beaten
1/4 c. warm melted butter (or fat)
2 pinches salt
2 pinches soda

Mix starter, cornmeal, milk, eggs and stir thoroughly in large bowl. Stir in melted butter, salt and soda. Turn into a greased frying pan or Dutch oven and bake for 30 minutes.

SOURDOUGH STARTER

1 qt. lukewarm water
1 pkg. dry yeast
2 tsp. sugar
4 c. all-purpose flour

Put water in crock; add yeast and sugar to soften. Stir in flour. Cover with a clean cloth. Let rise until mixture is light and slightly aged, about 2 days. Mixture will thin as it stands; add flour as needed. As you use sourdough from the crock, replace it with equal amounts of flour and water.

SOUTH OF THE BORDER CORN BREAD

1 c. self-rising cornmeal
1/2 c. self-rising flour
2 T. sugar
2 c. creamed corn
2 eggs, well beaten
1/2 c. bacon grease (or reserved grease from meat)
1 c. buttermilk
1 lb. ground beef
1/2 lb. pork sausage
1 lg. onion, chopped
4-5 tiny hot Mexican peppers, seeded and chopped
2 c. grated Cheddar cheese

Fry ground beef and sausage together until brown. Drain; reserve grease from meat. While meat is browning, mix together cornmeal, flour, sugar, corn, eggs, bacon grease and milk.

Pour 1/2 of batter into a lightly greased 13X9X2" pan, sprinkle with cornmeal. Sprinkle cheese over batter, then crumbled meat. Mix together chopped onion and peppers; sprinkle over meat. Pour over remaining batter. Bake at 350 degrees for 1 hour.

*Kate's Restuarant, Windslow, Arizona, 1955.

QUICK & EASY CORNMEAL CAKES

1 c. yellow cornmeal
1 c. cold water
1 tsp. salt, if desired
2 c. boiling water

Mix cornmeal, cold water and salt, then add gradually to 2 cups water boiling in heavy saucepan. Cook 5 minutes. Remove from fire. Pour into greased loaf pan. Cover to prevent crust from forming. Chill until set. Slice into 1/4-inch portions. Fry in buttered skillet, or use bacon drippings, just enough to keep from sticking. When golden brown on both sides, serve warm with butter and syrup, honey or molasses. Or you may prefer homemade jelly: prickly pear, wild grape or algerita berry. One loaf serves 4 or 5. If desired, add to mush while cooking: 2 tablespoons each, wheat germ, unprocessed bran and sunflower seeds.

CORN FRITTERS

3 eggs, separated
1 2/3 c. cooked or canned whole grain corn
1/2 tsp. salt
1/8 tsp. pepper
1/4 c. sifted all-purpose flour
6 T. fat or salad oil

Beat egg yolks until light, then add the corn, seasoning and flour. Fold in stiffly beaten egg whites last. Drop by spoonfuls into hot fat in skillet. Cook on both sides until brown. Serve with butter and syrup or jam.

JALAPENO HUSHPUPPIES

2 c. white cornbread mix
2 T. flour
3 eggs, slightly beaten
1 bunch green onions, about 6 stalks, chopped
1 white onion, chopped
1/2 c. milk, approximately
Salt and pepper to taste
1 T. jalapenos, chopped

Combine cornbread mix, flour and eggs. Add onions and enough milk to make the mixture tacky. Add salt, pepper and jalapenos. Shape, using a small round ice cream scoop and fry in hot oil until golden brown. Yields: 2 dozen.

RYE BREAD-SOUR DOUGH METHOD

15 c. rye flour, mixed with 5 c. white flour
1 1/4 c. lukewarm water
1 T. salt
1 1/2 T. sugar
2 cakes yeast or 1 c. ferment

For fermented sour dough, make up one or two days in advance. Crumble 1/2 cake yeast into 1/4 cup lukewarm water. Set this sponge in a warm place for a day or two. (This measurement includes water necessary for leavening.) Bread will keep fresh for a week if kept in a tin box or covered crock. Sour dough well mixed with the flour and lukewarm water and left to rise overnight has the power to raise the dough to double its bulk and produce sour but pleasant smelling sponge.

Stir half the flour into lukewarm water and add either ferment or yeast cakes crumbled in a small part of lukewarm water. Let stand, covered, in a warm place overnight. Next morning, add the remaining flour mixed with salt. Blend well. Place on a lightly floured board and knead until smooth and elastic but not sticky. Place in a large, greased mixing bowl. Cover and set over a pan of hot, but not boiling water or in a warm place such as the back end of a range. Let rise until double in size. Divide into 2 pieces and form 2 large loaves. Cover and allow to rise again to double its bulk over hot water. Place in slow oven as directed. Let stand overnight before slicing. Bake at 324 degrees for 1 1/2 hours.

SWEETS

CHRISTMAS HOLIDAY BREAD

4 c. flour, sifted
4 tsp. baking powder
1/2 tsp. salt
1 c. butter, softened
1 c. sugar
5 eggs
1 c. milk
1 c. seedless white raisins
1 tsp. grated lemon rind
1 tsp. vanilla
1/2 c. finely chopped nuts

LEMON GLAZE
1 1/4 c. confectioners' sugar
1 tsp. vanilla
4 T. lemon juice

In a mixing bowl, sift together flour, baking powder and salt. In a separate larger bowl, cream butter and gradually add sugar until mixture is light and fluffy. Add eggs, one at a time, beating after each addition. Gradually stir flour mixture into egg mixture, alternating with milk. Beat batter until smooth. Stir in remaining ingredients in order given. Pour batter into a greased 7-inch tube pan. Bake in moderately hot (350 degrees) oven 50-60 minutes. When done, invert pan and cool cake on rack. Cover with lemon glaze and decorate with citron and whole nuts.

Lemon Glaze: Mix ingredients until smooth. Spread directly on warm holiday bread.

BROWN SUGAR POUND CAKE

1/2 c. shortening
1 c. margarine
1 16-oz. box brown sugar
1 c. sugar
5 eggs
1 c. chopped nuts
3 c. sifted flour
1/2 tsp. baking powder
1/2 tsp. salt
1 c. milk
1 tsp. vanilla extract

Cream shortening, butter and sugars. Add eggs, one at a time, beating after each addition. Sift dry ingredients together. Combine milk and vanilla; add alternately with dry ingredients to creamed mixture, beginning and ending with dry ingredients. Beat well after each addition. Pour into greased and floured tube pan. Bake at 350 degrees for 1 1/2 hours.

GRANDMOTHER'S MOLASSES CAKE

1 c. shortening
1 c. sugar
1 c. molasses
1 tsp. salt
2 eggs
1 c. raisins and currants
Flour to make a soft batter
1 T. ginger
1 T. cloves
1 T. cinnamon
2 c. sour milk
1 tsp. baking soda

Cream shortening and sugar. Add molasses and beaten eggs. Sift dry ingredients and add alternately with 1 1/2 cup of sour milk. Mix the soda in the remaining milk and add with remainder of flour. Floured currants and raisins are added last. Bake in a loaf pan in a slow oven about one hour.

JOHNNY CAKE

1 1/2 c. yellow cornmeal
3/4 c. flour, sifted
1 1/2 tsp. baking powder
3/4 tsp. baking soda
1 tsp. salt
2 T. sugar
2 eggs, beaten
1 1/4 c. sour milk or buttermilk
1/4 c. shortening, melted

Sift flour, cornmeal, baking powder, soda, salt and sugar together. Combine eggs and sour milk (or buttermilk) and add to the flour mixture. Mix well and stir in the shortening. Bake in greased 8X8X2" pan, in moderately hot oven, 375 degrees, for 40 minutes.

SPICE LAYER CAKE

2 c. light brown sugar
1/2 c. shortening
2 eggs
3/4 c. milk
3 tsp. baking powder
1 c. chopped raisins
2 1/4 c. flour
1 tsp. cinnamon
1/2 tsp. cloves
1/2 tsp. nutmeg
1/2 tsp. salt

Cream sugar and shortening and beat until fluffy. Add the eggs and beat until light. Sift the flour, add salt, spices, baking powder, then sift again. Add the dry ingredients to the egg mixture alternately with the milk. Beat thoroughly and add the floured raisins. Pour into 2 greased layer cake pans. Bake in moderate oven, 350 degrees for 25 or 30 minutes. For the icing, use:

2 c. Sugar
3/4 c. milk
2 T. butter

Cream together and boil until it forms a soft ball when dropped in water. Add vanilla and beat until cold. Spread between layers, over top and sides.

SUGAR CAKES

3 c. sugar
3/4 c. butter
2 eggs
2 tsp. baking soda
1 c. thick milk

Mix eggs and butter well. Then add milk and soda. Mix in enough flour to make a soft dough, just so you can roll it. Cut into any shapes you wish. Sprinkle with granulated sugar, bake in a moderately heated oven.

BUTTERMILK CANDY

1 c. buttermilk
2 c. white sugar
1 tsp. soda
1 T. white Karo syrup
1 1/2 c. pecans
1/2 stick margarine

Bring to a boil the buttermilk, sugar, soda and Karo syrup. Boil hard for 5 minutes. Add pecans and margarine. Boil 5 minutes more (hard boil). Take off heat. Add **1 tsp. vanilla** and beat or stir 2 minutes. Drop with a teaspoon on waxed paper.

CHRISTMAS BUTTER COOKIES

1 c. soft butter
1/2 c. brown sugar, packed
2 1/4 c. flour, sifted

Cream butter until it resembles whipped cream and slowly add the sugar, beating well. Add flour gradually and blend thoroughly. Wrap in waxed paper and chill for several hours. Knead dough slightly on floured board; form into a smooth ball. Roll to about 1/8-inch thick and cut to desired shapes. Place on ungreased cookie sheets and bake in moderate oven, 350 degrees for about 12 minutes. When cold, decorate with butter icing, candied fruit, etc.

COWBOY COOKIES

2 c. sifted flour
1 tsp. soda
1/2 tsp. baking powder
1/2 tsp. salt
2 c. rolled oats
1 tsp. vanilla
1 c. granulated sugar
1 c. brown sugar, packed firm
1 c. shortening
3 eggs
1 6-oz. pkg. chocolate chips
1 c. chopped nuts, optional

Sift together and set aside flour, soda, salt and baking powder. Blend together sugars and shortening. Add eggs; beat until light and fluffy. Add rolled oats, vanilla and chocolate chips. Dough is crumbly.

Spread on lightly greased jelly-roll pan. Bake 20 minutes at 350 degrees or until done in the middle. Remove from oven and slice in bars.

FAMOUS OATMEAL COOKIES

3/4 c. vegetable shortening
1/2 c. granulated sugar
1/4 c. water
3 c. oats, uncooked
1 tsp. salt, optional
1 c. firmly packed brown sugar
1 egg
1 tsp. vanilla
1 c. all-purpose flour
1/2 tsp. soda

Preheat oven to 350 degrees. Beat together shortening, sugars, eggs, water and vanilla until creamy. Add combined remaining ingredients; mix well. Drop by rounded teaspoonfuls onto ungreased cookie sheet. Bake at 350 degrees for 12 to 15 minutes. (For variety, add chopped nuts, raisins, chocolate chips or coconut.) Makes about 5 dozen cookies.

MORMAN CHRISTMAS COOKIES

1/2 c. shortening
1 c. brown sugar
1 c. molasses
1 egg
4 c. flour
1 tsp. cinnamon
1 tsp. cloves
1/2 tsp. nutmeg
1 tsp. soda

Blend shortening, sugar and molasses. Add beaten egg. Sift dry ingredients and combine. Mix well, roll out and cut in fancy shapes. Bake at 350 degrees for 10 minutes. When cool, decorate with boiled icing.

MORMAN DARK COOKIES

1/2 lb. butter
1 c. sugar
1 T. cream
2 c. dark molasses
1 T. cinnamon
1/2 T. ginger
1/2 tsp. cloves, ground
8 c. flour

Cream the butter and sugar together until smooth. Add the cream, molasses, cinnamon, ginger and cloves and blend smooth. Work in the flour gradually. Roll out as thin as possible on floured board. Cut into various shapes with cookie cutters. Bake on greased cookie sheets in moderate oven, 350 degrees for about 12 minutes. Decorate, using a pastry tube and icing made from egg white and confectioners' sugar.

SHOO-FLY PIE

For the crumb part:
1/4 c. shortening
1 1/2 c. flour
1 c. brown sugar

For the liquid part:
3/4 tsp. baking soda
1/8 tsp. nutmeg
A little ginger, cinnamon and cloves
1/4 tsp. salt
3/4 c. molasses
3/4 c. hot water

Work the crumb ingredients together.

Mix well together and add hot water. Into an unbaked pie shell, combine the crumbs and liquid in alternate layers with crumbs on bottom and top. Bake 15 minutes at 450 degrees, then 20 minutes at 350 degrees.

PEACH DUMPLINGS

1 c. sugar
1 T. butter
1 c. milk or cream
2 c. sliced peaches
1 c. flour
2 tsp. baking powder
1/2 tsp. salt
2 c. hot water

Make a syrup of the sugar with the butter and 2 cups hot water. Add the peaches. Let this come to a boil. Make dumplings by mixing flour and baking powder and salt into a fairly stiff batter with milk or cream. Drop large spoonfuls of this batter in the boiling syrup and peaches. Cover and cook for 20 minutes. Serve while hot.

POTATO DOUGHNUTS

3/4 c. sugar
2 eggs
1 c. mashed potatoes
1 T. baking powder
2 1/2 c. flour
1 1/2 T. shortening
1/2 tsp. salt
1/8 tsp. nutmeg

Beat mashed potatoes, add melted shortening, beaten eggs and milk. Sift dry ingredients together and add to the liquid. Dough should be soft yet firm enough to roll. Separate dough into 2 parts and roll each out to thickeness of 3/4-inch. Cut with doughnut cutter and cook in deep fat, 365 degrees. Fry to golden brown. Drain on absorbent paper. Dust with powdered sugar or sugar and cinnamon mixture.

GRANDMA'S CRUMB OR SUGAR PIE

2 c. flour
1 heaping c. brown sugar
1 1/2 T. shortening
1 tsp. soda
1/2 c. buttermilk or sour cream
Salt
1 9", unbaked, pastry shell

Combine sugar, flour and soda. Cut in the shortening and blend well. Add the liquid and rub into coarse crumbs. Put crumbs loosely into the unbaked pie shell. Bake in moderate oven, 375 degrees for 40 minutes. This is a breakfast treat especially good for dunking in coffee.

ILLEF RANCH FAMOUS PIE

1 c. flour
3/4 c. sugar
1 tsp. baking powder
1/2 tsp. salt
1/3 c. butter or margarine
1/2 c. milk
1/2 tsp. vanilla
2 eggs
1 unbaked pie shell (in glass pie pan)

SAUCE

2 1-oz. squares unsweetened chocolate
3/4 c. boiling water
1 c. sugar
1/3 c. butter or margarine
1/2 c. chopped nut meats
Chocolate shavings (as garnish)
Whipped cream or vanilla ice cream (as garnish)

Sift together flour, sugar, baking powder and salt. Combine the butter, milk and vanilla; add dry ingredients to this. Beat 2 minutes. Add the eggs and beat 2 minutes longer. Pour into unbaked pie shell.

Melt chocolate in boiling water. Add sugar and bring to a boil. Remove from heat and add butter and vanilla. Pour sauce over pie batter; sprinkle nut meats over the top. Bake 55-60 minutes or until done at 350 degrees. Garnish with whipped cream or vanilla ice cream and shavings of chocolate.

*This delicious pie was brought west by John Wesley Illef's wife, one of her favorites.

LEMON CUSTARD PIE

2 T. flour
1/2 c. sugar
2 eggs, separated
Pinch of salt
1 lemon
1 1/2 c. milk
1 pie shell

Mix 2 tablespoons of flour with 1/2 cup sugar and a pinch of salt. Beat 2 egg yolks. Add the juice and grated rind of 1 lemon. Then add flour and sugar, continuing to beat. Stir in 1 1/2 cup milk and lastly fold in 2 eggs whites beaten stiff, but not dry. Pour into unbaked pie shell. Bake in hot oven, 425 degrees, for 15 minutes. Reduce heat to moderate, 350 degrees, and bake 15 minutes more.

SAUCES, GRAVIES, PRESERVES, CANNING AND RELISHES

SAUCES, GRAVIES, PRESERVES, CANNING & RELISHES

GUACAMOLE
(Avocado Dip)

2 T. finely minced white, mild onion
1 to 2 chilies, serranos
2 sprigs cilantro
Salt to taste
2 med. avocados
1 med. tomato, skinned, seeded and chopped

In a molcajete or blender, grind together the onion, chilies, cilantro and salt to a smooth paste. Mash the avocado flesh roughly with the chili paste in the molcajete. Stir in the chopped tomato and onion. If the guacamole is to be served as a dip, put it on the table in the molcajete.

BEAN DIP

1 can refried beans
6 to 8 oz. Montery Jack cheese
1 T. Jalapeno pepper or chopped green chilies
1/2 tsp. taco seasoning
3 T. tomato paste
1/4 tsp. garlic

Mix together and heat and stir in cheese and seasoning. Serve with Dorito chips.

TIP: Save cooking heat by remembering that cheese is an instant food. Eat it sliced or cubed with bread, crackers or fruit. If you need to melt it on burgers, meat loaf, on top of a casserole or in a sauce, the heat from the food is usually enough to melt the cheese.

NACHOS

Corn tortilla chips
1/4 lb. Monterey Jack cheese
1 or 2 Jalapeno peppers, diced finely

Lay chips out on a cookie tray. Place small piece of cheese on each chip. Top with a small piece of pepper. Broil in oven until cheese melts.

HOT JALAPENO DIP

11 1/2 oz. jalapeno pepper strips
16 oz. container sour cream
1/2 tsp. salt
1/2 tsp. paprika
1/2 tsp. cumin powder
2 8-oz. pkg. cream cheese, softened
Fresh parsley for garnish
Paprika
1 lg. bag Frito Lay corn chips

Drain jalapeno pepper strips and chop well. Combine sour cream, salt, paprika and cumin with jalapenos in a large bowl. Add cream cheese to sour cream mixture and blend until smooth. Pour into a decorative bowl. Chill before serving. Garnish with fresh parsley sprigs and jalapenos and sprinkle with paprika. Garnish with corn chips. Yield: about 5 cups.

CREAMY GARLIC DRESSING

2 c. mayonnaise
1 c. buttermilk
1 tsp. Accent
1 1/2 tsp. garlic salt
1 tsp. onion salt
1 tsp. parsley flakes
1 tsp. oregano
1/8 tsp. celery salt
1 tsp. dried chives

Mix all ingredients well. Refrigerate. This will keep a month or so. Great on salad or baked potato.

MINT SAUCE FOR LAMB

1/2 c. vinegar
1/4 c. sugar
1/4 c. water
1/2 c. finely snipped mint leaves
Salt to taste

In saucepan, combine vinegar, sugar, water and salt. Bring to boil, reduce heat and simmer, uncovered, 5 minutes. Pour immediately over mint leaves; let steep 30 minutes. Strain or serve as is, hot or cold, with lamb. I usually store it with mint leaves still in and strain into serving pitcher.

MUSTARD

1/2 c. wine vinegar
1/2 c. Burgundy wine
1/2 tsp. salt
2 eggs
1 c. sugar
1 c. dried mustard

Stir vinegar, wine and mustard; let stand overnight. The next day, beat the eggs and sugar until creamy. Combine all ingredients in a double boiler and cook until thick, about 30 minutes. Stir in the salt. Use as you would any mustard.

RAILROAD SALAD DRESSING

2 c. mayonnaise
1 c. catsup
4 T. Worcestershire sauce
1 tsp. paprika
4 T. vinegar
3 T. sugar
1 tsp. salt
1/2 tsp. garlic powder

Combine all ingredients; mix thoroughly and chill.

REAL TOMATO KETCHUP

1 gal. tomato juice or pulp (1 peck tomatoes makes 1 gal. juice)
1 pt. sharp vinegar
6 T. salt
4 T. allspice
2 T. mustard
1 T. powdered cloves
1 tsp. black pepper
1/4 tsp. red pepper

Put tomato juice into kettle and bring to a boil. Mix spices and vinegar in a bowl. Add to hot juice and let simmer until it is thick. The mixture must be constantly stirred or the spices will settle on the bottom and burn. If made from concentrated tomato juice, 1 1/2 hours of simmering is sufficient; but if made from canned tomatoes, the mixture should be allowed to slowly simmer for 4 hours. When the kettle is removed from the fire, let the mixture stand until cold. Then stir and pour into small-necked bottles. If 1/2-inch olive oil is poured into each bottle and the bottle is then corked, the catsup will keep indefinitely in a cool place. It is better if chilled before serving.

FRIED JALAPENO PEPPERS

1 egg
1/2 c. milk
1/2 tsp. Savory salt
2 T. Salad Supreme (This is an all-purpose seasoning made by Schilling)
1/2 tsp. garlic salt
2 c. any pancake mix
2 doz. jalapeno peppers
Deep fat or vegetable oil

Combine egg, milk and Salad Supreme. Beat well. Combine Savory salt, garlic salt and pancake mix in a separate bowl. Dip peppers into liquid, then flour. Repeat. Fry in deep fat or vegetable oil until they are golden brown.

INDIAN JALAPENO JELLY

1 med. red bell pepper
1 med. green bell pepper
1/4 c. jalapeno peppers
1 1/2 c. white vinegar
6 1/2 c. sugar
1 6-oz. bottle Certo

Chop all peppers very fine. Combine peppers, vinegar and sugar in kettle and bring to a rolling boil. Set aside for 10 minutes. Stir in fruit pectin. Let set 10 minutes. Pour into hot sterilized jars and seal.

Yield: Seven 1-pint jars.

INDIAN RELISH

14 ripe tomatoes
12 sour apples
7 small onions
1 sweet red pepper
2 T. salt
1 c. raisins
1 c. sugar
1 pt. vinegar

Chop all together the tomatoes, apples, onions, pepper and salt. Add raisins, sugar and vinegar. Let cook until thick and clear. Pour into sterilized jars and seal.

MAIN HOUSE HOT PEPPER SAUCE

1 c. oil
2 c. vinegar
2 c. sugar
1 32-oz. bottle catsup
2 tsp. salt
4 diced green peppers
1 gal. hot peppers (cut off tops, hull out seeds and slice thin)
1 head cauliflower, broken in small pieces
3 diced onions

In a large pot, bring solution to a boil. Add vegetables; keep turning until all are hot. Put in hot pint jars; seal. Makes 14 pints.

MAIN HOUSE HOT PEPPER BUTTER

3 T. salt
1 peck hot peppers
3 lbs. brown sugar
1 qt. vinegar
1 qt. mustard

Grind peppers in blender. Mix everything all together. Cook 25 minutes. Take **1 cup flour**, 1/2 with water to make paste. Pour in peppers. Cook until thick. Put in jars.

MARTHA LEE'S GREEN PEPPER JELLY

6 green peppers, cut in strips
1 1/2 c. white vinegar
7 1/2 c. sugar
6 oz. fruit pectin
1 hot pepper
Green food coloring

Put one-half peppers and one-half vinegar in blender ten seconds. Repeat until peppers are all blended. Put in large saucepan. Add sugar. Bring to a boil and boil for 6 minutes. Add pectin. Boil 3 minutes more. Add coloring. Put in jars. Makes 4 pints.

PEPPER RELISH

18 red peppers, stemmed and seeded
12 green sweet or bell peppers, stemmed and seeded
12 med.-sized onions, peeled
2 c. vinegar
2 c. sugar
3 T. salt

Grind peppers and onions. Cover with boiling water and let stand 5 minutes. Drain. Add vinegar, sugar and salt and boil 5 minutes. Pour into sterilized jars and seal.

RANCH CHOW CHOW

12 1/2 lbs. green tomatoes
8 lg. onions
18 green peppers
3 T. salt
6 hot peppers
1 qt. vinegar
1 T. cinnamon
1 head cabbage
1 T. allspice
1/4 tsp. cloves
3 T. mustard leaves
1 1/4 c. sugar
1/2 c. horseradish

Chop tomatoes, onions and peppers together and cover with salt. Let stand overnight. Add the hot peppers, which have been chopped, and add vinegar and spices. Allow to boil slowly until tender, about 15 minutes. Pack tightly in jars and seal at once.

TUCSON HOTEL SEASONING SALT

4 oz. celery salt
2 oz. garlic powder
1/2 tsp. paprika
1/2 to 1 c. sugar
4 oz. onion powder
1/4 c. chili powder
1 T. pepper

Mix together and add to **2 1/2 lbs. salt**. This can be used for meat like beef, pork or venison.

SALTED CORN
(A method of Preserving)

Cook the corn on the cob for 5 minutes. Cut off. To every quart of corn, add 1 cup salt. Mix well and pack in a crock. Cover cloth with a plate. Tie a cloth over the crock.

To serve, rinse and drain with hot water 4 times. Soak for about 5 hours before cooking.

*Salted corn is preserved by a very old method and is used very little today.

TO CURE HAMS

100 lbs. ham (from corn-fed hogs)
3 oz. saltpeter
1 pt. fine salt (best quality)
1/2 lb. brown sugar

Mix thoroughly the last three ingredients and rub over the hams and let stand for 24 hours. Then rub the meat with:

2 pts. fine salt
1/8 lb. black pepper

Let stand for five days and then rub meat again with fine salt. Set aside for 30 days. At the end of 30 days, hang the meat up and brush off the salt. Have hams smoked at a good smokehouse, smoking them for 10 days with wood. When finished, rub entire ham with red pepper. Wrap carefully in brown paper and then in muslin bags and hang up with the hock down. Hams prepared in this manner will keep indefinitely; flavor and quality improve with time.

TO PICKLE CURED BACON

100 lbs. sides of bacon (from fresh killed country hogs)
8 lbs. salt
3 lbs. brown sugar
3 oz. saltpeter
4 gal. spring water

Lay the sides of bacon on a board and rub lightly with fine salt. Let stand for 48 hours. Mix salt, brown sugar and saltpeter thoroughly and dissolve in the water. Bring to a boil and cook for 15 minutes. Skim and let cool. Place bacon in a clean oak barrel and pour the liquid over the meat. Place a heavy weight on bacon to keep it under the brine. Bacon prepared like this will keep about 1 year. Have sections of bacon smoked at smokehouse as needed.

TOMBSTONE PICKLED EGGS AND RED BEETS

2 c. (about 1 lb.) young beets
1/4 c. brown sugar
1/2 c. vinegar
1/2 c. cold water
1/2 tsp. salt
Small piece stick cinnamon
3/4 tsp. whole cloves
6 hard-cooked eggs

Wash beets; cut off leaves and stems, leaving on about 1-inch of the root end. Cook until tender. Drain and skin. Boil together for 10 minutes all remaining ingredients except the eggs. Let beets stand in this liquid for several days. Add whole, hard-cooked, shelled eggs to the liquid and let stand in refrigerator 2 or more days.

*Oriental Saloon, Tombstone, Arizona, late 1865. Saloon keepers used to give pickled eggs and red beets to patrons. Sometimes on weekends, cowboys would eat over 300 pickled eggs and beets or more. You can double or quadruple this recipe, depending on how well you like pickled eggs and beets.

BEEF JERKY

Cowboys on the trail drives or working large spreads usually only ate two meals a day which were breakfast and supper. They usually supplemented lunch with biscuits or corn cakes that the cook had left over and the most popular was beef jerky. Here's a common method of making jerky:

Dry beef; cut in strips as long as you can. It's best to cut against the grain. Cut strips about 1-inch so that meat will dry quickly. Cut off as much fat as you can. Sprinkle each piece of meat with salt and pepper and a small amount of chili powder. You can hang the strips of meat in a dry place or on wire lines. It's best if you have a full sun, but a shed or smokehouse will do fine. Do not hang where the jerky has a tendency to draw dampness. Just be sure the jerky does not get wet. When the jerky looks and feels like an old shoe leather, remove from its drying place and store in flour sacks or large jars. Sometimes it might have a little mold on it when it ages, but a little vinegar and water will remove the mold and it's just as good to eat.

GREEN CHILE EGGS

3 T. butter
8 eggs, well beaten
3 T. milk
4 drops Tabasco sauce
1/2 c. green chilies, chopped
Salt to taste
1 tsp. paprika
1 c. sour cream

Heat butter in a heavy skillet. Combine eggs, milk and Tabasco sauce, whip to blend well. Add chilies to eggs, stirring well. Pour into heated butter, cook like scrambled eggs. Sprinkle eggs with paprika and salt. Serve with a bowl of sour cream. Serves 4.

HOMEMADE SAUSAGE
This is spicy-like the cowboys liked!

10 lbs. ground pork scraps
5 tsp. salt
2 1/2 tsp. dry mustard
5 tsp. black pepper
2 1/2 tsp. ground cloves
5 tsp. ground red pepper
6 1/2 T. ground sage

Mix the seasonings and then work them thoroughly through the meat. Sausage meat may be packed loose for freezer storage or it may be stuffed into natural casings, plastic or cheesecloth and stored in the freezer or smoked.

*This recipe was given to me by a friend I rodeo'd with who worked at the King Ranch, Globe, AZ.

SALOON-STYLE CLEAR GRAVY

Butter well the inside of a saucepan. Cover bottom with **thin slices of onion.** Lay **some 1/4-inch-thick slices of fresh (not smoked) ham** on top of the onions. Add **3 pounds veal knuckles, 2 pounds shank soup beef and bones, and some cooked or boiled chicken carcass bones.** Add **2 cups brown sauce, 4 quarts consomme** and bring all to a vigorous boil for about 30 minutes, skimming all the while. Reduce heat to a simmer; salt to taste. Add **8-10 whole peppercorns, a bunch of parsley, 3 bay leaves, pinch of thyme** and a **clove of garlic.** Allow to simmer for about 5 hours. Strain through a fine sieve and allow the liquid to cool slightly. Skim off all the remaining fat. Strain through a cloth and it is ready for use. This will keep in a refrigerator for 4-5 days.

This recipe may be cut in half to make up suitable amounts for different sized families. Excellent to serve with roast beef or steak or other meat dishes.

*Most all cowboys like gravy; most all of your old saloon cooks made gravy. I have about 10 recipes for saloon-gravy but this is basically the old-type saloon-style gravy. Try it—it's delicious. Sure beats the hell out of eating packaged gravy you can buy at the stores today or what my wife can make!

INDEX

Regional Ranch & Pioneer Cooking 5
Arizona Apple Dumplings 7
Baked Spareribs with
  Sauerkraut Dumplings 7
Arizona Farm Pancakes 8
Arizona Hush Puppies 8
Arizona Molasses Taffy 9
Arizona Teriyaki Steak
  with Onions 9
Arizona Boiled Tongue 10
Sauce for Boiled Tongue 10
Desert Chicken Fried Steak
  with Country Gravy 10
Flavorful Beef and
  Black Bean Salad 11
Grand Canyon Steak 11
Green Pepper Steak 12
Homer's Iron Skillet Special ... 12
Rodeo Pork with Onions 13
Saloon Beans 13
Sourdough Steak 14
Canyonland's Cabbage 14
Chicken Livers with Apples
  and Onions 15
Desert Rice 15
Ethel's Stewed Chicken
  and Dumplings 16
Hotel Turkey Casserole 16
Old South Arizona Spiced
  Chicken 17
Papago Roast Pheasant Stuffed
  with Grapes and Nuts 17
Arizona Salad 18
Phoenix Steak 18
Canyon Sugar Beans 19
Desert Land Potato Salad 19
Old-Ranch-Style Beans 20
Papago Sweet Potato
  Cakes 20
Ranch Style Frijoles 21

Scottsdale Baked
  Cabbage 21
Arizona Kelly's 7-Bean Soup .. 22
Arizona Pot Stew 23
Bean Kettle Soup 23
Cowboy Beef Stew and
  Dumplings 24
Globe Chuckwagon Bean
  Soup with Beef 24
Flagstaff Hunter's Stew 25
Mormon-Style Beef Soup
  with Dumplings 25
Mormon-Style Pork Pot Pie
  with Dumplings 26
Oriental Saloon Stew 26
Poor Cowboys Stew 27
Red River Bean Soup 27
Sheepherder's Brown
  Potato Soup 28
Trail Wagon Beef Soup 28
Venison and Wild Rice Stew . 29
Canyon Land Meatloaf 29
Cookstove Meat Loaf 30
Grand Canyon Meatballs 30
Prescott Stuffed
  Green Peppers 31
Ranch Style Meat and
  Cabbage 31
Company Ham 32
Flagstaff Scrapple 32
Herb-and-Garlic Marinated Leg
  of Lamb 33
Pioneer Red Eye Gravy 33
1855-Style Sauce 33
Spanish Omelet 34
Arizona Stockyard Special
  Ham 35
Special Ham Sauce 35
Bunkhouse Turnips
  and Pork 36
Shorty's Spareribs and
  Roast Potatoes 36

115

Sauerkraut and Pork 37	Navajo Peanut Soup 57
Pioneer Hash 37	Navajo Yam Cakes 58
	Papago Baked Pumpkin 58
Mexican & Indian Cooking .. 39	Pima Cactus Salad 59
Mexican 41	Pima Crispy Fried Fish 59
Arizona's Best Fajitas 41	Pima Fry Bread 60
Beef Mexicana 42	Pima Huckleberry Bread 60
Gazpacho 42	Pima Fry Bread 61
Chicken Fajitas 43	Pima Fried Hominy 61
Enchiladas, Arizona Style 43	Pima Fry Bread 62
Fiesta 44	
Frijoles (Refried Beans) 44	**Bar-B-Q and Chili 63**
Guacmole Senora	**Bar-B-Q 65**
Widener 45	Grand Canyon Barbecue
Beef Tacos- Tucson Style 45	Sauce 65
Just Plain 'Ole Fajitas 46	Barbecued Chicken 65
Mexican Chicken 46	Best in the West Bar-B-Q
Mexican Bean Soup 47	Ribs 66
Mexican Salad 47	Holbrook Barbecue Beef or
Mexican Fiesta 48	Pork Ribs 67
Mexican Corn Tortillas 48	Ace High Barbecue Sauce ... 67
Mexican Wild Tortilla Soup ... 49	2-C Ranch Barbecue
Old Style Enchiladas Ole' 49	Sauce 68
Old-Style Wheat Flour	Mustard Dip 68
Tortillas 50	Arizona's Favorite Barbecue
Quick Style Frijoles Refritos	Sauce 69
(Refried Beans) 50	Hot and Spicy BBQ Sauce ... 69
Outlaw Beef Burritos 51	Dry BBQ Sauce 70
Taco Salad 51	Black Jack BBQ Sauce 70
Queso Tortillas 52	Original Hot Sauce or
South of the Board Salad 52	Barbecue Sauce 71
Indian 53	Barbecue Salt 71
Apache Acorn Stew 53	Barbecued Goat 72
Apache Charcoal-Broiled	Arizona's Best Stew or BBQ 72
Buffalo Steaks 53	Barbecued Pork or
Apache Fried Rabbit (Wild) . 54	Beef Roast 73
Apache Squirrel Stew 54	Pioneer Mustard Short Ribs ... 73
Hopi Baked Sweet Potatoes and	Wittenburg Beef Kabobs 74
Hickory Nut Sauce 54	Barbecue Slaw 74
Hopi Indian Corn 55	Bull Rider's Slaw 75
Hopi Lamb Stew 55	Tombstone Hot Beans 75
Indian Charlie's Indian	Restaurant Salsa 76
Pudding 56	Real Hot Taco Sauce 76
Indian Chestnut Bread 56	Trail Boss Salsa 77
Indian Pudding 57	Quick Green Chili Salsa 77

Chili **78**
  Pecos Bill's World Championship
    Chili Recipe 78
  Sheepherder's Chili 79
  Triple C Chili 79
  Wild Card Chili 80
  Chili Fiesta 80
  Cactus Chili 81
  Sheepherder's Chili 81
  Yuma Chili 82
  Arizona Cotton Chopper's
    Chili 82
  Flagstaff Hotter Than
    Hell Chili 83
  Arizona Mex Chili 83

Breads & Sweets **85**
Breads **87**
  Arizona Biscuits on a Stick 87
  Beef or Pork Biscuits 87
  Cornmeal Biscuits 88
  Old Style Baking Powder
    Biscuits 88
  Corn Bread Stuffing 89
  Pappy's Skillet Corn Bread 89
  Poor Charlie's Sourdough
    Corn Bread 90
  Sourdough Starter 90
  South of the Border Corn
    Bread 90
  Quick & Easy Cornmeal
    Cakes 91
  Corn Fritters 91
  Jalapeno Hushpuppies 91
  Rye Bread-Sour Dough
    Method 92
Sweets **93**
  Christmas Holiday Bread 93
  Brown Sugar Pound Cake 93
  Grandmother's Molasses
    Cake 94
  Johnny Cake 94
  Spice Layer Cake 95
  Sugar Cakes 95
  Buttermilk Candy 96

  Christmas Butter Cookies 96
  Cowboy Cookies 97
  Famous Oatmeal Cookies 97
  Morman Christmas Cookies .. 98
  Morman Dark Cookies 98
  Shoo-Fly Pie 98
  Peach Dumplings 99
  Potato Doughnuts 99
  Grandma's Crumb or
    Sugar Pie 99
  Illef Ranch Famous Pie 100
  Lemon Custard Pie 100

Sauces, Gravies, Preserves,
*** Canning & Relishes*** ***101***
  Guacamole 103
  Bean Dip 103
  Nachos 104
  Hot Jalapeno Dip 104
  Creamy Garlic Dressing 104
  Mint Sauce for Lamb 105
  Mustard 105
  Railroad Salad Dressing 105
  Real Tomato Ketchup 106
  Fried Jalapeno Peppers 106
  Indian Jalapeno Jelly 107
  Indian Relish 107
  Main House Hot Pepper
    Sauce 107
  Main House Hot Pepper
    Butter 108
  Martha Lee's Green Pepper
    Jelly 108
  Pepper Relish 108
  Ranch Chow Chow 109
  Tucson Hotel Seasoning Salt 109
  Salted Corn 109
  To Cure Ham 110
  To Pickle Cured Bacon 110
  Tombstone Pickled Eggs
    and Red Beets 111
  Beef Jerky 111
  Green Chili Eggs 112
  Homemade Sausage 112
  Saloon-Style Clear Gravy 113

If You Would Like To Order The

Original Arizona Cookin' Cookbook or *Original Cowboy Cookbook*

Send a card with name and address and $13.50 plus $2.00 for postage and handling to:

Original Arizona Cookin'
%Record Printing Co.
PO Box 530 - 214 High St.
Cairo, NE 68824

OR

Phone:
1-800-658-3241